THE
ANGRY FILMMAKER
PRESENTS

ANOTHER
KELLEY BAKER
JAG

Gretchen,
Follow your dreams,
and get the sound right!

Angrily yours,

Kelley

3/20/10

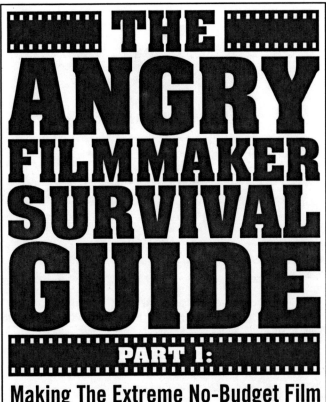

THE ANGRY FILMMAKER SURVIVAL GUIDE

PART 1:
Making The Extreme No-Budget Film

KELLEY BAKER

(AKA: The Angry Filmmaker)

PO | PISSED-OFF
And Not Going To Take It Anymore

ANGRY FILMMAKER

Angry Filmmaker, Inc.   PO Box 8322   Portland, OR 97207

AngryFilmmaker.com

To order additional copies, please contact us.
BookSurge
www.booksurge.com
1-866-308-6235
orders@booksurge.com

ISBN: 1-4392-3273-3
EAN: 9781439232736

To My Father,
who has never lost faith in me,
and has always been there.

For Kid
The One who keeps me going.

I was in love with the notion of making an independent movie. I didn't pay attention to the part of me that kept saying, What if this doesn't work out? What if people don't help you?

I had successful people all around me, and a good track record with my short films.

What could go wrong?

—*Kelley Baker*

ACKNOWLEDGEMENTS

I want to thank Fiona Baker for being my light in the dark. Don Campbell who came up with this dumb idea in the first place. Brian Johnson for tirelessly discussing it with me, and for his help and support over the years. Jeff Pollard for all of his great artwork, and for always being around to get "ship wrecked". Margie Yap for showing me the way, and hanging on to my dream when it got too heavy. Diana Powell my brilliant copy editor, for taking the thoughts in my head and helping me make sense of them. Book store Doug Hawkins for always encouraging the "dark" stuff. Josh Cross for pushing me forward. Tom Laswell for teaching me how important good actors are, I still miss you. Tim McHugh for always having a couch. Ricardo Moore, "cause it's not easy...", and Harris Mattarazzo for keeping me out of debtors prison.

I also want to thank Jim & Mary Baker, Concha Solano, Randy Timmerman, Nicky Silverstone, Teresa Tamiyasu, Don Alder, Mary Chris Mass, Jean Dresler-Ameele, Debby Dietrich, Pete Dresler, Jay Tormohlen, Cari Callis, Danny Boyd, Marty & Robin Oppenheimer, Kim Blair, Brian Berg, Michael "Gonzo" Gandsey, Al Lee, Leslie and Jamie Baker, Bruce Lacey, Rocky & Bullwinkle, Drop Kick Murphy's, Pabst Blue Ribbon, Dan Cox, Pete Townshend, Gary Lacher, Peter Appleton, Wayne Woods, David Cohen, Alexander 23, Terry & Kathy Peterson @The Dockside, Patrick Winters, Richard Beer, Ellen Bergstone Beer, John Flenniken, Gerry Lewis, Harry B Miller III, and Mel Sloan.

To all of the casts and crews I have worked with over the years. With out all of your hard work people would be looking at a blank screen. You all helped bring my vision to life. Thank you.

EXECUTIVE BOOK PRODUCERS

24 People Who Should Really Know Better by Now!

Brian Johnson & Kate Ertmann
Pam Parker
Harris Mattarazzo
James Baker
Richard Moore
Alexis Halmy & Al Lee
Earl Sutherland
Mary Bauer
David Fechtor
Jill Colburn
Paul Diener
Cathy Zeitlin
Lesly Verduin
Jim Carrier
Andrew Holtz
Aaron & Cheryl Olson
Arati Moses
Steve Finnegan
Paul Sabal
Richard Beer
Tim Maffia

Without their support this book would never have made it
to the printers. Thank you all. Your copy is in the mail.

THE SHIT:

MORE SHIT:

FORWARD

By Cari Callis

Kelley Baker's energy and "anger" burns up the theater. He visited Columbia College Film and Video Department in 2005 and gave a presentation to about 200 students from Screenwriting and Sound classes. The students loved his wit and humor and most importantly, he inspired them with the possibilities for their own films. Kelley makes it all look like fun as he talks passionately about his process and the struggles to get his own films made and marketed. He provides our students with a unique perspective of what a filmmaker has to go through to work outside of any sort of corporate system. His ideals and stories of working within the studio system are hilarious and brutally honest. After his lecture and screening the students mobbed him to buy his films and to talk to him. Kelley spent another hour answering their questions and talking about everything from his writing process to mixing sound for Gus Van Sant.

Sometimes our students forget that low budget filmmaking is all about following your passion and telling stories that rattle people's cages. Kelley reminds them to do both. We're bringing him back this semester for an encore performance and as a guest lecturer for several classes. We want to support what Kelley stands for in the filmmaking community, a story telling rabble rouser with a soul, but mainly we're inviting him back because the students loved him and were inspired to make more films!

Cari Callis
Writer, Filmmaker, and
Screenwriting Professor, Columbia College

PREFACE

By The Angry Filmmaker

I am the poster boy for bad decision making in the Independent Film world!

I have made eight short films, three features and a couple of documentaries, along with a ton of corporate videos, and commercials. I have whored myself on other people's movies for the last 20+ years. There are certain truths I have learned, and certain things and people I shouldn't have listened to.
I have messed up my life financially, emotionally, and probably physically and it's all been for my love of movies. My movies.

A lot of people ask me why I'm angry. I am the Angry Filmmaker after all. What makes me angry is the state of **INDEPENDENT** films. The independent film industry is no longer even remotely independent. It's been mainstreamed by Hollywood and is now simply another over-hyped product. Like commercial radio, pop music and Starbucks coffee, the industry has become a homogenized mess of conglomerates owned by a handful of extremely powerful corporations. It begs the question: Independent from what?

We need to take the word "Independent" back!

Indie has become a marketing phrase. I have a tough time sitting through a ten million dollar "indie" movie. I want people to recognize that "indie" doesn't mean stars and all of that other crap. WE are Independent Filmmakers" and WE make movies whether WE have a deal or not. I want to see more theaters and media art centers providing places for us to show our work, instead of just giving us lip service about how they support independent film. I am fed up with these "independent" film festivals that show all these movies with big names in them. I think Sundance and any other film festival that calls themselves independent shouldn't take films with budgets of more than $100,000. That ought to weed out the phonies...

For me, filmmaking is all about the work. All about the movie. If making a movie is just one of those things you think would be cool to do, then don't do anything. There are already enough posers and bad movies out there. We don't need anymore.

But if you are like me, if making your movie is the most important thing, then keep moving forward. I always tell people that making a movie is a lot harder than you think. And if making a movie was so easy, there would be a lot more movies out there. But making a movie is hard! Making a good movie is even harder!

I make my films because I have to! I have stories I have to tell and I won't be satisfied until my movie is done, and out.

I love movies. I always have. When I was a kid I used to watch just about anything. In fact one of my guilty pleasures is still running across *Dirty Dancing* on cable late at night. I've probably seen it fifty times. I have always wanted to meet Jennifer Grey, even though I understand that she was just playing a role and she's had surgery on her nose and all of that stuff. She was fantastic (and really hot!) in that movie. She means more to me than Carrie Fisher with the bagels strapped on her head in *Star Wars!* Jennifer, are you out there?

When I first went to USC's Film School, I really wanted to make movies like the ones that I grew up watching. I still remember going to the movie theater and seeing movies like, *Grand Prix, Easy Rider,* any Clint Eastwood Western, *Bullitt, How The West Was Won.* They were amazing. I remember being mesmerized in those old theaters.

My first day in Film School the instructors went around the room asking us what kind of films we wanted to make. I was a poor kid from Oregon who was feeling like I didn't belong there. Everyone in my class talked about all of these great art films, and foreign Directors, and how they wanted to make these personal statements. They were all "Artists" and scaring the hell out of me. When it was my turn, I said that I wanted to make movies to entertain. I had no great mission, no great statement.

The Instructors totally wrote me off as some one with nothing to say and my films were not taken seriously for the first year. Then it happened...

After studying the films of Fritz Lang, Orson Wells, Howard Hawks, Sergio Leone, Billy Wilder, Frank Capra, John Cassavetes, the list goes on and on. I realized that film was so much more than I thought. It wasn't just a way to tell a story (which is still important); it was a way to truly communicate with an audience. To use film as a way of saying things. To protest, to educate, to enlighten. I realized that some of the films about the Korean War were really about Vietnam, just set in a different context. So many of these great directors had things to say. It's a pity that so many of today's directors don't.

I know that I was naive and intimidated in film school, but the joke is that these people that were in my class, the ones who wanted to be "Artists", and had so many things to say, went into the industry (those who survived film school), and worked on all sorts of bad movies. Low budget crap that in many instances went straight to video.

Where was the "Art"? I wondered. Was this my first lesson in filmmaking? Were all of those people in my class there for the same reason I was? To learn to make entertaining films? Did they just say that "art shit" to BS the instructors and get better grades? I'll probably never know.

I fled LA after I graduated. I had this belief that true

"independent" filmmaking was what I wanted to do. I spent years learning my craft, working on other people's movies, and soaking up everything I could. I started making short films first, then graduated to features.

I have been to film festivals, financing conferences, and the Independent Feature Film Market, three times! So many of the films I saw were financed by the people who made them. Many of them had glossy production values, but no stories. They looked like so much of the crap coming out of Hollywood.

After panel discussions that would feature employees from the so called "Indie" Distributors, (Fine Line, Miramax, Fox Searchlight, etc), I witnessed the audience attack these people like piranha! Everyone was desperate to talk to a real distribution executive and to pitch their projects. I saw the panelists being polite, but they weren't interested. Unless you had William Macy and Parker Posey and had spent ten million dollars they weren't going to look at your movie.

Many of the filmmakers had a look of desperation on their faces. They had spent way too much money! Their own money!

Too many people finance their films on credit cards, and they go broke! Their films end up not getting a distributor and they're left paying 30% interest on a film that no one wants. Heed the words of noted financial consultant and former NBA player, Charles Barkley, "Credit cards exist to keep poor people poor."

DON'T USE YOUR DAMN CREDIT CARDS FOR ANYTHING!!!

Does that mean I've never funded something with credit cards? Yes! And I have lived to regret it. Not the eventual movies, but the financial shape it left me in. I sold my home of twenty years to get the IRS off my back, all because I listened to the wrong people. People who said they would help me. I was gullible because making movies is all I've ever wanted to do. I am now debt free, and homeless. So please, don't do what I did. The stress isn't worth it.

The Angry Filmmaker's Survival Guide seeks to restore order to this once venerable filmmaking arena by providing young, new and even old-hand, jaded and bitter filmmakers with a practical guide to independent filmmaking. In that I qualify as an "expert" by any acceptable or measurable standard, my book offers not only practical, step-by-step, easily accessible information about the craft, but it offers plenty of attitude about the state of the world of Independent Film.

I make the films I want to make at a cost that doesn't break the bank!

When no one else wanted to distribute my films I started doing it myself. I found that the best way for me to get my films out was to tour. The touring lifestyle can be a lot of fun, and it can be brutal.

It is like being a punk band on the road, with no punks and no music. Just the road... There are times when I wake up and have no idea where I am. And sometimes late at night on dark highways you mind plays tricks on you. But you know what? I wouldn't trade any of this for anything.

What I have learned is that if you do something, you need to go all the way. Go big, or go home!

So, read this book, and if you have the guts, you too can become a true "Independent" filmmaker and show your films all over the world. Or you can be a sell out and go to Hollywood and make *Police Academy 54.* It makes no difference to me.

If you truly want to go the independent route, hang on. It's going to be a very scary ride...

CHAPTER 1:

Understanding Film

"No one gives a shit if you ever write a script or make a film. No one cares! But if you do, then keep writing and making films. Ultimately, you're the only one that matters."

I'll be brutally honest: Not everyone should make a feature film. In fact, most people should merely watch them and dream. But if you're convinced that a major feature is your future, it's imperative that you start with short films, to learn your craft and build a track record. Remember, if you're going to blow money you might as well start with a little and then work up to blowing millions. Ask Michael Bay (*Pearl Harbor, The Island*) about blowing millions and having nothing to show for it.

We all love movies. Movies play a huge role in our lives. People try to emulate some of the things they see on screen, which is all well and good if you're watching a movie like *Norma Rae*, or *To Kill a Mocking Bird*, not so good if you're watching *Jackass: The Movie,* or *Friday The 13th Part 42*.

Why you should make shorts first

Ronald Reagan used to have trouble distinguishing history and his own reality with the movies he was in. He never served in

WWII, yet talked as if he had been there because he had made a war movie or two. Movies shape the way we look at the world, and movies shape the way the world looks at us. People watch my short films and feel they know me. Maybe. Or maybe they just know a part of me. The part I wish to share.

Watching a movie is much easier than making one. So most of you should just put this book down now and forget about it. Why? Making a movie is not just grabbing your video camera and shooting. A lot of people try that and their movies usually suck. It's going to take time, lots; patience, even more; and the ability to move mountains, on a good day.

We are going to start with short films here because that's what you should start making first. If you make a feature without ever having made a short film, you're an idiot! Filmmaking is as much a craft as it is an art form and a business. First and foremost, you have to learn your craft.

MAKING THE SHORT PERSONAL FILM

We are all voyeurs.
We like bad things to happen ... to other people.
We enjoy watching it.

What are personal films? I can tell you what they aren't: THEY ARE NOT YOUR HOME MOVIES! Nobody cares about your vacation slides, and they certainly don't want to look at Fat Aunt Alice at the beach. Please don't make us look at that.

Personal films should have some sort of universal appeal. They should contain something that we can all identify with.

All of my films are personal, whether they're shorts or features. They're slices of my life, they're a part of me. In the short films, it's all out in the open for people to see. In the features,

2

they're hidden as composite characters or events.

What is it about my life, or a vignette from my life, that others can relate to? Is it my sense of humor? My bizarre take on life, or just a really weird incident in my life?

Don't think for a moment that personal films are only seen at film festivals, the Internet, or screened just for your friends. Some personal films have gone on to do respectable numbers at the box office. Some of these films you've seen before, some you haven't. I say get your butt down to a video store and see these things. If they're not at your local video store then you're renting from the wrong place.

Examples:
- a. *Sherman's March, Past Imperfect, and Time Indefinite* (Ross McElwee)
- b. *Silverlake Life: The View From Here* (Peter Friedman & Tom Joslin)
- c. *Roger and Me...* (Made back when Michael Moore actually cared about what he was doing)
- d. *Monster in a Box, Gray's Anatomy, and Swimming to Cambodia* (Spalding Gray)

These are all features and documentaries, and they are admirable. In my opinion, however, personal films should be short films. It's hard to sustain other people's interest when we're talking about our own lives. If you are going to bore an audience, bore them for a short time.

I was dumb enough to appear in my own short films. I could never find someone who could play me, so in addition to learning the craft of writing and directing, I learned a lot about being in front of the camera. Something I have not done since my shorts. I respect actors and work with them a lot better now that I've seen it from the other side.

Angry Filmmaker's note: There was an interview years ago where George Lucas was talking about this little "independent" and personal movie he was making with Francis Coppola. How it was just something they wanted to do and so they were doing it, all on their own, outside the Hollywood mainstream. The little movie he was talking about was *Tucker*, with a 25 million dollar budget. You guys can kiss my ass! A *25 million dollar* little independent movie? What kind of crap is that? The movie sucked. The ending was upbeat, unlike the story in real life. I hate it when these idiots talk about their little "personal" projects. These guys are so full of shit.

But I digress.

First and foremost, like I teach in my Low Budget Feature workshop, make your idea fit the budget. Don't write something you can't pull off. How much money do you have? (*25 million dollars?* Don't get me started.) For my first film I had no money, but an urgent need to tell a story.

I didn't like being in front of the camera, ever. It was bad enough to pull some of these things out of my life and put them up on the screen, but to have me up on the screen too... I was really uncomfortable with all of it. I did it because I needed to get some of these things out of my system. I don't have a big ego (wait a minute, yes I do). I couldn't find anyone who could play me. Now, I would be lying if I didn't say that sometimes people come up to me at airports (it's happened) or festivals or wherever and say that they recognized me from one of the films. That was nice. But on the whole, I wish someone else was in them.

So if you're going to do these kinds of films, you need to ask yourself, "Am I the best one to be in this film?" If you are, then go for it. If not, DON'T DO IT! We have all seen too many films with a writer/director/star that truly suck. Especially first-time filmmakers. Most of them can't act, write, or direct, let alone do all three!

When you have to direct yourself, it's a bitch! You can't watch yourself while you're acting. You have to judge takes on how you feel about what you just said, and what your camera person tells you. This is tough. Maybe you need a co-director for these kinds of films. (Although, how do you split a vision?)

I've never liked co-directors. I'm not a fan of collaborators in general (I don't play well with others) because one person usually ends up doing the majority of the work. In my case, it usually ended up being me, and that has hurt many a friendship.

If you can find someone that you can truly collaborate with, don't fool around, marry them! Forget the film business, just go off and be happy!

As the director/star, and in some cases the producer, you have to look out for lots of things. In addition to everyone's performance, you're worried about locations, food, people arriving on time, and having all of your props. This is why I like short films. If you treat every short film as a one-day feature shoot, you're going to learn a lot more and be better prepared when you move up to longer projects.

Angry Filmmaker's note: Remember, if you piss off your crew, you'll never really know it until you're back in the editing room. That's when you will see things like the boom, or mic shadows, or that the focus is soft. Don't ever piss off your camera person! You will live to regret it.

So you really want to do this?

Then first check out other people's personal films. What did they do right, and what bores the hell out of you? Figure out why some of these films are successful, and why others aren't.

In the case of ***Roger and Me,*** Michael Moore made up this persona of the "everyday Joe." He's a nice overweight guy with a baseball cap, just asking questions. In his earlier films, he played dumb. In his later films, he can't get away with it. We all know who he is, which I believe was always his intention. But are his films really personal? I don't think so. He always has ulterior motives. Plus I'm tired of him. Don't get me wrong, I respect what he's doing. It's just that his shtick is wearing thin.

Ross McElwee, on the other hand, is great. I never get tired of him. In his movies he really is an "ordinary guy" who deals with issues we can all relate to: relationships with women, family, the outside world. Who the hell are we? Who are these others we're attracted to? Or related to? Why does it all matter? (I'm not sure either, Ross, but you really make me think. I actually got to meet him once and was impressed. Nice fellow. The kind of guy you want to go out with and have a cold one. So if you're ever in Portland, Ross, give me a call. I've got this great place we can go hang out.) Watch all of his movies, he does it right. And why he's never had any mainstream success is beyond me.

Since this is my book, I figure I should talk about my short films. I'll tell you why I did what I did. The mistakes I made, and the smart things I did. As a point of reference, in my opinion, a short film is from two to ten minutes in length. I hate twenty-five minute short films. They are usually ponderous and always need a good editor. If you are going to make shorts, make them short.

A buddy of mine told me that talking about your first film is like talking about your first girlfriend: it takes guts. Well, let's see how brave I am.

That Really Obscure Object of Desire

This was my first short film, outside of school. The one that started it all. I made it because I was pissed. And my sister, Leslie, was pissed, at me. In my family we don't communicate very well. So I made a film.

It was supposed to be shot in a single day.

I had an old 1928 Model A Ford that my Father gave me for my fourteenth birthday. I said that I was going to fix it up. Well, I never did. It was sitting in my parent's driveway rotting away while I was living in LA, attending film school. When Mt. St. Helens erupted in 1980, it spread ash, and other crap, all over the Northwest, and that included my car. When I was home visiting that summer, I decided I needed to store the car inside somewhere, so I started looking around.

Leslie recently bought a house with a nice garage, and I thought it was the perfect place. I didn't ask her (that's how it works in my family, like I said, we don't talk), but she had a feeling that something was going to happen, so she started taking the bus to work and leaving her car in the garage. I didn't know this, so I hired a tow truck to take the car over there. Needless to say, when I found her car locked in the garage I was stuck. The tow-truck driver dropped the car in her driveway and left.

Leslie came home, and boy, was she pissed! She came around the corner, and there was this rusty, rotting hulk of metal in the middle of her driveway for all her neighbors to see. The next day, she left me the keys to her car. I was able to get it out of the garage and my car in. The only thing she said was that I had 6 months to find a new place for my car. I went back to LA the next day.

Six years later... I received the final ultimatum.

Leslie was out of town when I hired another tow truck to remove the car, to another free garage I'd found. I decided I was going to make a film about moving the car, and I would interview her for it. I forgot to tell her about that part. She came home in the middle of the shoot, not feeling well, but she was so happy about the car being moved that she agreed to an interview the following weekend when she felt better.

And thus, a style was born.

The tow truck driver turned out to be a great guy with a real sense of humor. He explained everything he was going to do before he actually did it and then waited while we set up the camera. He ended up working with us most of the day even though his radio kept going off and the dispatcher wondered why it was taking so long. This was my first foray into going over budget, but certainly not my last. The tow was supposed to cost me $35. It ended up costing $75 because it took so long, plus I tipped the guy.

I shot 1200 feet of 16mm film and spent what little money I had on film processing and work printing. I did all of the picture and sound editing myself.

At the time, I was making a living editing other people's movies and doing sound work as well, so I already had a background in it. I don't recommend editing your own work unless you've done it on other people's movies. As an editor you need to remain objective, something that's easy to do on other people's movies. It is much easier for me to tell someone else that a scene they directed is garbage. It's much harder to look at my own work and tell myself that.

I did a sound mix at a facility in town long after they had closed for the day. It took 4 hours to mix it, but my friend the rerecordist told his bosses it took 45 minutes and that was my bill.

I was so excited about this film. When it was finished, I immediately sent it out to every film festival I could find and eagerly awaited their response, knowing that my career was about to be launched.

After being rejected by every film festival, I was dejected.

It costs money to enter festivals, and I had spent a lot. I got letters back saying that my film didn't fit in with their film festival, but thanks for the money, or something like that. I couldn't believe it didn't get into one single film festival, not even the local one.

I've since learned a lot about film festivals and how they work, or don't. More about that later.

The film sat on my shelf for over a year while I completed work on my first documentary, *Criminal Justice*. *Criminal Justice* follows three cases through the courts: a rape, a robbery and a homicide and what really happens behind the scenes. I didn't know what to do with *That Really Obscure Object of Desire.*

I sent *Criminal Justice* around and had a little luck in festivals. One day I was reading The Independent, and saw a call for films for a series on PBS. They were paying an amazing amount of money per running minute on any programs they bought. But I had missed the deadline.

Deadlines? Who cares? I called the producer anyway and told him that I knew I had missed the deadline but I had this amazing 60 minute documentary. He said he'd look at it, but I could tell he wasn't that interested. "Did you have anything else?" he asked. Just my failure. I told him about *That Really Obscure Object of Desire.* He got excited and told me about a movie he made about his car, *Winter Beaters* or something like that. Long story short, he bought the short film.

That Really Obscure Object of Desire aired nationally on PBS in a series called *American Pie,* and I got lots of notoriety. I had a meeting at KTLA in Los Angeles, and when I walked into their programming department, a couple of people came over and introduced themselves. They loved my film. I was sort of a cult figure to them. All I had to tell people in the PBS system after that was that I made a movie about my car for *American Pie.* They would usually start laughing and tell me they loved that short. It opened a lot of doors for me.

After being rejected by lots of film festivals, my movie was seen by a couple hundred thousand people on a single national PBS airing, and they paid me. Who was laughing now?

Don't give up on your movie. If you believe in it, you will find someone else who believes in it too. It just might take a while.

The question I'm asked most often about my short films is: What was scripted, and what was "off the cuff?"

Everything is scripted! You have to plan and organize. I want them to feel off-the-cuff, but you need to know as a filmmaker what the hell is going to happen. I think this is true whether you're doing documentary or dramatic films. The tow-truck driver was great because he told us what he was going to do before he did it. He allowed us some quick set-up time. The only part of the shoot I didn't have completely worked out was the different angles I wanted to cover. Having the driver explain to us, in advance, each step as he was doing it allowed us to cover the shots that I wanted.

As I said before, I look at short films as a single day of a feature shoot. I want to get everything lined up and done right, so that I'm not wasting anyone's time. When you're doing your short films, you need to know exactly what's going to happen the entire day. Morons who say, "I just shoot and capture what happens," aren't filmmakers. They are observers. Filmmakers plan things and have contingency plans for the unexpected.

You'll Change

When I made *You'll Change*, my second short, I had to plan everything out because I needed to shoot it in a single day. There are two reasons for this:

One is that your friends are working as your crew, and you need to respect their time. Most industry professionals don't have a problem donating a single day to help, but ask for more, and that's tougher.

The other reason to shoot an entire film in a single day is (as I will keep repeating), it's great training for low-budget features. How much can you get done in a short amount of time? Trust me, that knowledge and ability helps when making features. I know how fast I can move a crew and how quickly I can do multiple camera set-ups. I also know that if I shoot outdoors I can get more shooting done than if I have to light an interior. Unless, of course, the weather is bad. Then what?

I intentionally set my films in the winter in Oregon when the weather is totally predictable. It's gonna rain. I use the rain to help me set mood. There is no such thing as canceling because of rain on any of my movies. It doesn't happen. It never will.

On *You'll Change*, I asked myself, "Can I really do this on only two 400-foot rolls of film?" It's all talking heads, how can I make it interesting? I need to do eight locations in a single day. Can I make that happen? Where are my locations? Do I need permission? Can I get away without permission?

You'll Change was made for around $500. It was a direct result of all my friends bothering me about having my first kid at thirty five years old. Yep, those really are friends of mine, and they knew their lines before we shot. Most of the guys were taking breaks from their jobs.

Since I had no budget, I had to make sure that everything went smoothly and that no one blathered on. Everything had to be nailed down. I kept my locations close to each other so we never had to drive far. I also picked places that I wouldn't have to worry about as far as getting permission, or pay for parking. The crew was small enough that everyone and our equipment fit into one car. Since I was driving, no one got lost.

The first two interviews I shot were interiors. I realized after the two interviews that I was behind schedule. There was no way I could get all seven guys shot in a single day if we had to light every interior. So everyone else was shot outdoors. We used some reflectors, but with some of the locations we didn't need to add light. When it's all cut together, no one knows what was shot when. This is a lesson I learned well and continue to use on all of my films.

I shot less than 700 feet of film (about 20 minutes worth) for a final version of 3 minutes. All of the film stock was free. It was nothing but short ends, leftover rolls of film from commercials and other projects that had been stored in my refrigerator.

How do you get free film? I would call up commercial and corporate production companies to see if they had any out-of-date film stock they were going to throw out. If a commercial production company were to shoot a paying job on old film stock and there were problems with the film at the lab when it was processed (faded color, light leaks, whatever), they would look pretty stupid to their clients. How do you explain to a client that is paying tens of thousands of dollars that you're using out-of-date film stock? The smart companies don't do it. Many production companies would have refrigerators full of old film. Some of them would even call me when they had stuff to get rid of. I shot just about all of my short films on out-of-date film stock. If stored properly, it'll last years after its expiration date.

Now, with digital video, people aren't making shorts on 16 mm like they used to, but a lot of commercials and infomercials are still being shot on film. If you want to do a short on film, find out who these production companies are, and see if they want to donate some old film for your cause.

You'll Change was my breakthrough. It has shown everywhere. There was one PBS station that bought it every year to air on a single day: Father's Day, which was during their pledge week. I'd get anywhere from $300- $500 for the day. They'd air it at various times all day!

It has played all over the U.S., Europe, and Australia.

Not bad for $500.

I submitted it to lots of film festivals. Lots! And it got in. Soon, I had festival directors calling me. "We saw your movie at such-and-such film festival, would you care to submit it to our film festival?"

Here's the deal. If someone wants me to submit my film to their festival, what do I get in return? Fee waiver? T-shirt? Publicity? *If they're calling you, they need to give you something to get your film.* They can't ask you to submit, then charge you! That's bullshit! I always asked them to waive all fees, and they always did. They saw the film, knew it was good, and that's why they wanted to show it.

My next film was...

Stolen Toyota

This film was made for around $800, and has probably returned a couple hundred thousand dollars to me in grants, film festivals, TV airings, and commercial jobs. It was screened at film festivals, by PBS affiliates, and on Canadian and Australian television.

Why did I make this film? I was pissed! My car was stolen, and I felt personally violated. I shot the stuff at the wrecking yard not knowing what I was going to do with the footage. The rest of the movie was written and then shot in a single day, also on out-of-date film stock. It was edited in a day, and the audio was mixed in a few hours late at night.

Are you starting to see a pattern here?

There is a myth that Jim Jarmusch shot his first feature, Stranger Than Paradise, on nothing but short ends left over from a Wim Wenders film that he had worked on. I don't know if it's true or not, and if I ever get to meet Jim, I'll ask him. It served as an inspiration to me.

A friend of mine has often said, "Don't ask, don't get!" So now, I look at my films this way. What can I hustle? How many things can I ask for before I get too embarrassed to ask for more? Well gang, the possibilities are unlimited. I will ask practically anyone for anything. And more often than not, they'll say yes.

I shot the wrecking yard scene first. When the police called and told me they found my car, it wasn't drivable. I called two friends, (who happen to be industry professionals), Peter Appleton (camera), and Steve Miller (sound). I explained to them what was going on and that I wanted to have them film me at the wrecking yard the first time I see the truck. I had one

14

400-foot roll of film (about 12 minutes) to shoot. Since I didn't know what was going to happen, I didn't want to waste much film, and money.

Angry Filmmaker's note: One of the things I see in people who shoot video is they don't know when to turn the camera off! Tape is cheap, so they just shoot and shoot. There is no discipline! When we shot film, every roll was expensive, so we shot only what we felt we needed. Pretend that tape is expensive. Don't just shoot. Know what you want to get and shoot only what you want. It will save time while you're shooting and time in the editing room because you won't have to watch a bunch of useless shit! You can always tell some one who used to shoot film and is now shooting video. They turn off the camera in between shots. They don't leave the camera running when they are trying to focus. They don't waste tape, which saves time.

I didn't know who owned the truck next to mine in the wrecking yard. I saw that it was trashed and I talked about it. Everything was off the top of my head! I made sure that in addition to the shots of me talking, I shut up long enough to get some cut-aways. You can always use cut-aways.

Then I went home, processed the film and endured what I had to: settling up with my insurance company. As the process got weirder and more frustrating, I realized I might have a story. I contacted a few people I knew who had their cars stolen. Their stories were also weird. I wrote them all down and wrote a script based on what they said and what was happening to me. Then I started telling people that I was making a movie about my truck being stolen. One of my friends had a friend whose truck was stolen around the same time as mine. You guessed it! She owned the yellow Toyota that I had filmed in the wrecking yard. I met her and added her story to my script.

I wanted to do something more interesting than just boring

15

talking heads. I came up with angles that symbolized the people or their predicaments. I shot Terry in a parking lot full of cars where hers was stolen; to show her car was one of many. I shot Susan from above as she told me she felt quite small when she was dealing with the insurance company. Carol was shot outside the police impound lot where she spent a lot of time. Are you seeing what I'm doing here?

Besides, I wanted to make things more interesting visually, which is why we did the outline and the crime tape around where the truck had been sitting. I wouldn't compare car theft to a death in the family, but you do feel a loss. You also feel violated.

The sound at the wrecking yard was awful! We did the best we could since the location was literally right off a main highway. We were using a shotgun microphone, and I was trying to keep as far away from the road as possible, but sometimes you're stuck.

I checked out all of the other locations for sound before we shot. I always want any of my locations to be as quiet as possible. I prefer adding the sound later.

Stolen Toyota is easily my most popular film. Why? Every time I have screened this film, someone in the audience either had their car stolen, or someone close to them had. What a wonderful world we live in. Car theft appears to be rampant in this country.

In the end, the insurance company is the bad guy. Insurance companies are among the real villains in our society, right or wrong. Every year our insurance goes up. We have to pay it, and we get less and less service. (The insurance company raises my rates, and I didn't do anything wrong?) There are two things we all dislike. One, something being stolen from us, after faithfully paying our insurance companies for many years, and two, having them get the last word. They come up with all sorts of reasons not to pay out, or to pay much less.

There is something in **Stolen Toyota** that we can all identify
with. Remember this as you're making your films. You want the
audience to be able to make a personal connection to your work.

Somewhere along the line, in addition to getting phone calls
from film festival programmers, I got a call from the head of
programming at a Canadian television station in Toronto. She
had seen my films at film festivals and wanted to purchase
them. She also wanted to know if I had any other films she
hadn't seen. I told her she had seen everything. But...

I said that I had three other ideas. I made up the three ideas
right then and made it sound like they were all ready to go.
None of them were scripted. They weren't even close.

As soon as we started talking, I told her I would send one-page
treatments of what I had, and if she liked them, we could go
from there. I stayed up late that night writing one-page
treatments.

After a few more conversations, this woman commissioned three
films for a lot more money than I would have spent if I would've
funded them myself.

Always have an idea ready to pitch. Always!

Enough With The Salmon

This was the first film completed for Canadian television.

Most of us have some sort of memory about growing up and
family vacations. Good, bad or indifferent. Our tragedy is
always someone else's comedy. I was lucky that my father had
an 8mm movie camera and documented some of this stuff. But

as you see in the movie, he didn't use the camera enough to ever get comfortable with it. Watching it, you probably think I'm making fun of my parents, and I am. They actually really like this movie.

Doing a road movie is really hard! Parts of this film were shot at the same time as *Tales From I-5*. On both films, I was denied a location. I scripted the film and the various locations I wanted based on my father's old 8mm home movies, but trying to figure out exactly where they were, who owned them, and all sorts of things like that were easier said than done.

I traveled to the House of Mystery, which is an old beat-up house. Where it sits, things appear to roll uphill, and other parts of the house distort your perception. I don't remember the explanations behind why things happen the way they do, but as a 10-year-old kid, I thought it was pretty cool. The name was good too. I planned to shoot next to something that looked like it was rolling uphill.

I ended up shooting outside the House of Mystery because they wouldn't let us in with a camera. At the time, I couldn't remember what was so cool about the place, so I just made the whole thing up. We shot on public property with the sign in the background. If we hadn't driven sixty miles off of I-5 just for this one damn shot, I wouldn't have shot anything there at all.

Angry Filmmaker's note: All my personal films were shot on film. Video was around then (I'm not that old), but I didn't own any video equipment, only film stuff. Since I was still using short ends (as compared with dog ends) and had my own Nagra (reel-to-reel tape recorder), and 16mm transfer machine, I was making these films for the cost of the film processing and printing. If video had been prevalent then, I probably would have shot them on tape. It's a hell of a lot cheaper, and tape keeps looking better and better. Sorry, Kodak.

Now you can get an amazing video camera for just a few thousand dollars and really bad editing programs on the internet, so that's what a lot of people are doing. Some of them are making bad personal films. If you don't believe me, check out Yahoo, MySpace, and YouTube. There are tons of sites that show bad movies.

What these filmmakers are not doing is paying attention to story!

The writing chapter is coming up; don't miss it. Personal, documentary, long, short, experimental, it doesn't fucking matter! You still need to have something to say, and say it so it's understood. Even "experimental" films and videos have to have something about them that makes them cohesive. When these "experimental" artists make shit that's personal and no one understands it, they're just beating off. It makes no sense in anyone's world, so why watch it? Experimental work should still retain its own logic.

Let's get back to our story shall we?

Tales From I-5

This film was shot at the same time as ***Enough With the Salmon.*** You try keeping two absolutely different thoughts straight in your head while you're sweating your ass off in a 1979 Toyota Corolla full of equipment. That's why everything was written down. I was bouncing between both movies, trying to remember what piece was going to be shot where. I had made a list and I kept referring to it throughout the entire trip. I approached it just like shooting a feature out of sequence.

The weird thing about both of these films was that while I was on the road shooting, I suddenly got extremely depressed about my divorce and my life in general. I didn't eat much the entire trip. I just wasn't hungry. So the pain I was revealing while eating pea soup in 100-degree heat was real.

You can't plan moments like that.

One of the challenges with *Tales From I-5* was there were only
two of us doing everything. My faithful friend and cameraman
Gary Lacher and I were the entire crew. I was also the cast.
I mean, how many people can you fit with all of your gear in a
Toyota Corolla and drive over 1,000 miles, each way?

When we would shoot, Gary and I would figure out the best
place for me to stand where we wouldn't need to use any lighting
or reflectors (since we had no one to hold anything and no
power). Gary would set up the camera, I would set up the
recorder, do a test on my audio, Gary would put the headphones
on, I'd start the Nagra, run to my spot, do the slate, hide the slate,
and then start talking. Each shot took quite a bit of coordination.

On this trip we had two cameras with us. A CP-16 and an old
Bolex spring-loaded, wind-up camera, which we used for the
nonsync shots. The Bolex was a lifesaver. It was small, and we
could take it into restaurants, down on the beach in LA, or hang
it out the window of a fast-moving car. No one paid that much
attention to it.

One thing I've learned over the years: when I'm shooting and
I don't have permission or permits, I want to look like an
amateur. I am making a home movie. That way no one bothers
me. And on this movie we were really left alone. After being
denied permission to shoot in two locations early on, we started
using the Bolex and going where we wanted and getting what
we needed. Very politely and innocently, of course.

There are times when you should ask for permission, but on this
trip I re-learned the old adage: It's sometimes better to ask for
forgiveness, than permission. If I look like I know what I'm

doing, people will assume I have permission, and won't question me. We took this piece of knowledge and used it constantly on the making of **Kicking Bird**, my third feature.

I did have to check with my lawyer on one thing. I wanted to share my bout with food poisoning, and he told me that under no circumstances could I mention the name of the restaurant chain, because they could possibly sue me. (This was before **Super Size Me**, so I must say that I made fun of an unnamed fast food company first.) I did find out I could stand in front of their sign and talk about the incident and not mention their name.

This film was difficult because I knew where I was going to shoot most of it, this was a one-shot deal driving down to LA, and sometimes I had to improvise. The script was written, and I was worried that I wouldn't be able to get some locations.

As it turned out, I couldn't get one of the first locations. It was a small restaurant near Grants Pass, Oregon. I asked the owner about shooting in front of her place, and had one of the most bizarre conversations of the whole trip. I should have realized that there was a religious vibe over the place. The conversation, which I recount in the film, takes place in a rest area a few miles south of the restaurant. It's another reason to use a smaller camera and look like amateurs.

Love the One You're With

I don't like this movie. I was in a rush to finish it. I think I failed.

Here's what went wrong. Too many wide shots. I had been working with a lot of real people, and this was my first outing with actors. I'd never dealt with someone playing me, and I don't think I figured out how to do it at this point. Not everyone in the movie was an actor, but enough of them were, so I really had to work. I went on this shoot unprepared. Not enough time spent in rehearsals. I was making up the shots as I went along: not a good thing.

I had locations set up, but I hadn't broken the script down into shots. This wasted a lot of everyone's time. Even though it was shot in a single day, it should have been shorter!

When you are making a film, I believe you have to give it your all. This one was feeling like an obligation. I needed to get it finished, otherwise I would not be paid. I hadn't come to grips yet with my divorce and everything else that was going on in my life.

I was also tired of the short-film format at this point. I had made a bunch of them, and I had done everything I had wanted to do with the form. This was the last film I owed Canadian television. I was not in a good place mentally, and I think the film shows it.

This film did well on the festival circuit, and I get lots of requests for it. Go figure.

Friday Night

This film was shot on 600 feet (18 minutes) of film roughly 72 hours after I was released from the hospital. I think it's my best short film, because it's so raw. I also hate watching it, because it brings back too many bad memories. I almost died from an allergy shot. I went to the emergency room and went into anaphylactic shock. It was a story about fighting to stay conscious, and knowing that I could die at any moment.

The entire shoot took less than an hour. I was still very weak. I went into my studio, called up Peter Appleton (who has shot a lot of my short films and commercials) and Wayne Woods (who has been doing location sound for years), and arranged for them to come by the studio around 1 pm and shoot something with me quickly. Since Wayne was on his lunch hour and Peter was running errands, I promised them it wouldn't be long. I hung a piece of black velvet against a wall, set up one key light, loaded the camera, and set up the Nagra.

The day before, I had written everything I could remember about what happened. When Peter and Wayne arrived, I told them what we were going to do. Neither said much. We just did it. My hat is off to Peter for this film. I told him to just listen to the story as I was talking, and move the camera anyway he felt was appropriate. I told them I could probably only tell the complete story once, then we could go back and pick up some lines here and there. We had one chance at this movie, because I didn't know if I had either the physical or emotional strength to pull it off for very long.

The look was very important to me. I used the black velvet background because I knew it would absorb all the light that hit it. I would get a true black. Since I was only using a single key light to illuminate one side of my face, I wanted the stark contrast. Without using a fill light or a back light, my face emerges from the darkness, and at times appears to be edging into the darkness. Given the subject matter, I felt that the look was appropriate: me fighting against the darkness that may or may not envelop me. When we timed it later, I also added a blue filter, so the whole film had a coldness that symbolizes death.

I did the story once. The tears you see in the end are real. I took about five minutes to compose myself. Then we went back and picked up a few places where I thought there could be problems. They never said much during the shoot, and it wasn't until a few months later that Peter and Wayne separately told me how awful I looked, and how freaked out they were by the whole thing.

I spent years making funny films, and then came this one, which isn't funny. This film became a problem because of other people's perceptions of who I was and what I did. People didn't want to watch it. They wanted me to be funny again. This film was rejected by lots of film festivals. I was feeling a certain sense of deja vu.

The year before I made this film I was invited to the Eugene (Oregon) Film Festival, where they showed *Stolen Toyota* as part of their opening night gala. At the party afterward, many people came up to me and told me how much they liked my film.

The following year they asked me to come again, they had selected *Friday Night* for their opening night. I was flattered, being asked two years in a row. *Friday Night* played to a packed and very quiet audience. At the party afterward, the few people who came up to me told me how much they liked *Stolen Toyota* the year before. *Friday Night* makes people uncomfortable.

It did well, however, in European film festivals. This film helped open up the European market for me. That's another market to look at. Many stations in Europe still program shorts, and they like things that are "American." And believe me, there is nothing more "American" than cars, insurance companies, and our messed up medical system. Plus, they like movies that make you think about stuff like death. I don't know why, they just do.

No one in Europe ever asked me why I don't make funny films anymore. They look at *Friday Night* as an extension and an exploration of what I'm doing. I like that. They're a lot more liberal in an artistic sense than Americans are. They allow their filmmakers to grow and change as they mature.

Here's what I learned after making these seven short films: If you're going to do a short film, make it SHORT. I've met all sorts of people that make twenty five minute "shorts." They do it as a calling card to get into features.

The problem with these films is they're too long to do anything with. The odds are you are not going to get a feature deal from Hollywood based on your short. You need to try and recoup some of your costs; beyond that, you need to get your movie seen. Twenty five minutes is an awkward running time.

Here's the deal, film festival programmers, people who make short film compilations, and programming people at TV stations in other countries are all looking for real shorts -- the three to ten minute variety. Why? They can use them where they have holes in their programming. They call them "filler."

They're not going to show a twenty-five minute film before a feature (usually), and they're certainly not going to fill a hole in programming with a twenty-five minute film. But a five minute short? They can put that anywhere.

That's why my short films make money. I send them everywhere and will take modest sums for them. They can be shown in almost any time slot. They're truly short, mostly funny, and easily programmable.

I can do five or six short films for what many people spend on a twenty-five minute film. It means I'm learning a lot more about my craft, and I have five different films out in the real world working for me while other people only have one. This enables me to get my work seen by more people, which, in turn, can lead to more opportunities to recoup my costs.

Angry Filmmaker's note: What is this BULLSHIT about people wanting to broadcast your short films for FREE? Your films are worth something. It is NOT an honor to have it broadcast for FREE! It's a rip-off! If anyone (outside of film festivals. A different kind of rip-off) wants to show your film, they should have to pay for it! They need to give you something. I know a filmmaker who gave her work to the local PBS station, and if others want it, she'll let them have it for free! (She does have a husband who supports her in quite a grand manner, but I'm sure this has nothing to do with anything.) I told her that by doing what she's doing, she's screwing all of us.

Why? Because the local PBS station now feels entitled NOT to pay us for our work. She set a bad precedent. And she gave me shit about how I should let them have my films for "local exposure," that it's good for the community. FUCK THAT! It's a rip-off! My films didn't play locally for years because they wouldn't pay for them. Do you tell a doctor to take out your appendix for free and you'll tell everyone what a good job he did? That'll sure help him locally. I think not! We are professionals and we deserve to be paid just like everyone else. Anyone who gives their work to a broadcast entity for FREE is hosing all of us.

But more about distribution later. When I calm down.

So what is the central theme in my short films? My life and all its weird components, that for some reason, many people can identify with.

I Think I Was An Alcoholic

This was my last short film. It was made with a buddy of mine, John Callahan. John is a quadriplegic cartoonist whose work is absolutely, positively, politically incorrect. It's also damn funny! John is the first person to tell you that he is an alcoholic, and many of his cartoons are about his own problems. *I Think I Was an Alcoholic* started life as a personal memoir in cartoon strip form. It is John's story, and after watching some of my short films, he decided he wanted to do one of his own.

John and I previously collaborated on another short film based
on one of his cartoons, *How Much Is That Window In The
Doggie?* It was a one minute short -- basically a one liner.
It had done well in a few festivals and was featured in one of
Spike & Mike's Sick & Twisted Animation Festivals.

We had been friends for a while when we decided to take on
Alcoholic. There were certain things that I insisted on if we were
going to make this movie. The biggest thing was John would
have to narrate the movie himself. It was something that for him
was very difficult. He still complains about how hard it was.
I felt it was truly important to do it since the film was about him.
Not only is it John's story, but he is actually telling it. This is
what makes the movie as powerful, and as funny, as it is.

We made the film for about $8,000. It's all animated, so that
took money to hire someone to do the drawing and the shooting,
all in 35mm. For me, this was a huge budget.

This film is always a crowd pleaser, and it's doing well in the
educational market. It was sold to alcohol treatment centers,
colleges and universities all over the country.

It appeared at Sundance and at Annecy, a huge animation film
festival in France. I went to Annecy and found out that puking
in any language is funny. There are two animated puking
scenes, and even though many people in the screenings didn't
speak English, it still brought the house down whenever the
character was puking. And we like to think that Europeans are
so sophisticated.

I was the producer, as well as co-director with John Callahan and
Laura DiTrapani. I was okay collaborating with other people on
this film because it wasn't my story. Although I must say there

were still moments when I would get really annoyed asking questions and waiting for someone else to make a decision. But that was more my problem than anyone else's. I also knew this was going to be my last short film. By this time I had said everything I wanted to say in the short-film format.

There are a few people (actually a bunch of them) who keep telling me I should return to the short film format, but there is nothing I have to say. They keep telling me they miss my funny movies, and why can't I make funny movies anymore? I make the movies that I want to make. I never intended to make funny short films, it just turned out that way.

It was now time to tackle bigger things, and we all know what that means.

The first feature...

CHAPTER 2:

SCRIPTING, SCRIPTING, and more SCRIPTING

"You can't make a movie if you can't write! Unless you're George Lucas, or James Cameron, or ... oh, just forget it!"

I still say, you can't make a GOOD movie unless you can write and tell a good story. And box office grosses don't count. Some of the worst scripts have made a fortune at the box office. That's all about marketing, and what Abraham Lincoln said about "fooling some of the people all of the time". The Hollywood studios are fooling people. Don't believe me? Did you pay to go see any re-make of a bad '70s television show? A lot of people did.

Would someone please explain to me that last **Star Wars** trilogy? The writing is God-awful!

So many people I know said they knew it was going to suck. They know Lucas is a bad writer (not much of a director either). But they had to go see it. I can see going once, but EIGHT TIMES?! What is up with that? I mean, I know that some of us grew up with **Star Wars,** but we also grew up with chickenpox and you don't see people running out to get that? And believe me, **Star Wars** is a pox! I don't care what Lucas says. We'll see more episodes as soon as he realizes no one wants to see his other stuff. *Star Wars* is his ATM.

So let's get back to business.

Software makes the writer

"What kind of software do you use?" is the most frequently
asked question and possibly the stupidest one I've ever heard.
Software doesn't write your story, you do! The software doesn't
fucking matter! It's what's in your head that matters! Can we
just get past this?

Okay, I actually use WordPerfect whenever I write anything.
I love that program because it was designed for morons. I have
a full page on my screen, and I know what all of the buttons do.
Since I know screenplay format, I just write my scripts and then
format, manually. Why? Because you shouldn't be sweating the
mechanics of your software while you're writing. You should be
able to write effortlessly and then go back and do your
formatting.

Whatever you use to write, your formatted script should look
like this:

EXT - RUNDOWN HOUSE - DAY

MARTIN comes running around a corner. He runs up the stairs
of a house that has almost no paint left on it, the porch looks half
rotted. There are empty beer cans and whiskey bottles strewn
around the yard. Next to the porch is an old beat up Ford pickup
that's got primer spots all over it. It has a fancy set of wide tires
and wheels on it. On the back window it has a sticker that
proudly states: PROTECTED BY SMITH & WESSON.

This is MARTIN'S home. MARTIN leaps across the porch in

two strides, opens the door and is inside the house as the THREE JOCKS stop right in front of the house. One of the JOCKS is TOMMY BENSON, who's known MARTIN since grade school. HE's a tough kid, the kind who likes to pick on kids that are smaller than he is. HE and MARTIN have always hated each other, and no one can ever remember why. TOMMY's khaki pants have a huge brown stain on the front of them.

                    TOMMY (shouting)
          YOU'RE DEAD MEAT BIRD! TOMORROW
          YOUR ASS IS MINE!

                    JOCK #2
          We'll be waiting for you loser...

                    TOMMY
          I'M GONNA KILL YOU...

JOCK #3 grabs TOMMY by the arm.

                    JOCK #3
          Let's get the fuck outta here before that crazy
          old man comes out waving a
          gun again...

                    TOMMY
          I'm not afraid of these cocksuckers...

                                             CUT TO:

INT - HOUSE HALLWAY - DAY

MARTIN is leaning against the door listening to the JOCKS outside. HE hasn't even broken a sweat. HE smiles. WE hear a VOICE from off-screen.

                    GRANDPA (OS)
Marge! Is that you?

                    MARTIN
No Grandpa, it's Martin.

                    GRANDPA (OS)
Where the hell have you been?

                    MARTIN
                    (to himself)
Getting a fuckin' education...

                    GRANDPA
What?

                    MARTIN
School...

                    GRANDPA (OS)
Well get me a beer...

                    MARTIN
Yes Grandpa.

MARTIN looks out the window and watches the JOCKS walk
away.

Software Confessional

Angry Filmmaker's note: I was just given a copy of Movie
Magic Screenwriter 6 from my buddy Chris at Write Brothers.
I am impressed and amazed at this program. He told me
I would be writing within 15 minutes of downloading the
program. He was wrong. It took me about 20 minutes. I also

downloaded two early screenplays I have been rewriting and it formatted everything perfectly. It also has some tools I really like. From here on out I am sticking with Screenwriter.

I was told that there's script writing software that helps you with story lines. What's up with that? Are we that dumb, or uncreative that we have to depend on a computer program to write our scripts for us? Maybe we are.

When it comes to character names, I like to combine the names of kids I went to elementary school with, or teachers that I hated (that's you, Dave). It's my own fun little game. Just don't be too obvious, like killing your former principal or ex-girlfriend. They see through those things.

There are some good books out there about screenplays, and screenplay format. There are also some really bad ones. I promise I'll put a list of available books that at the end of this one, but I won't vouch for any of them unless someone pays me.

I used some of these books to learn the rules, then I started writing. Everyone talks about the three-act structure, character arc, having certain things happen at certain points in your screenplay. Some people say that a character has to learn something by the end of a story. Maybe. If you look at episodes of the old sitcom *Seinfeld*, those characters were never any smarter at the end of a show than they were at the beginning. Those characters never learned anything from their experiences. That was the point.

Over the years, I developed my own style and made up my own rules. It works for me. I'm not sure it works for everybody. You really do need to learn the rules of good writing and story telling, and then break them!

Angry Filmmaker's note: I will recommend The Elements of

Style by William Strunk, Jr and E.B. White. Still my favorite book on writing and style.

Think about the French New Wave. Those filmmakers were writers and critics first. They studied films, wrote about them, and then made their own. Truffaut and Godard (to name two) broke a lot of rules. It was refreshing. If you want to know more about the French New Wave, look it up on the Internet, and rent their movies. You will see some great stuff. Stuff that hasn't been shown on TV. By the way, their films are mostly black & white and usually subtitled, so you are going to have to work a bit.

Writing a Screenplay in Three Easy Steps

1. Put your butt in the chair. A screenplay doesn't write itself. You need to sit down, clear your desk and your mind. Then start writing. It takes commitment. Personally, I make myself sit down every day to write. I psych myself out. I only have to write a single page, then I can stop. And why not? If I just write a page a day, then in less than four months, I have a screenplay. How easy is that? Or, I just have to sit and stare at the screen for an hour. No matter how much I write, I can get up after an hour and do other things.

Sitting down to write is not rocket science. If it's a habit, and you set up the same time every day or every other day to do it, then you feel bad when you don't. So you do it. Simple, right? Make writing a habit!

My lawyer and his wife throw a Christmas party every year, and I am the token artist. The party is made up of people that we went to school with. I suffer through it every season because I like and respect my lawyer and his wife. I wish I could say that about some of the other people there. For me, not being very social, it's a pain in the butt.

This woman I'd never met came up to me and asked, "You're *the filmmaker* aren't you?" I said yes, and she introduced herself. She then proceeded to tell me that when she was in college, she used to write all the time. But now that she is married, has kids, and a ten-hour-a-*week* job, there just isn't enough time to write.

I just stood there, noncommittal, like I'd never heard any of this before. Then she said, "You're going to give me the lecture, aren't you?" "What lecture?" I said. She said I was going to tell her that if she really wanted to write, she'd do it. She'd get up earlier in the morning, or stay up late at night, or do it while the kids were at school. If writing was that important to her, she'd find a way. And she should find a way. She needed to write. When she finally finished with her little speech she looked at me and said, "That's what you were going to tell me, right?"

I said, "No." I told her I didn't give a shit whether she ever writes again. It doesn't matter to me. She's one less person that I have to compete with, and one less person whose work I might have to read. I don't care if she *ever* writes.

I never waste my time lecturing people who claim they "used to write." You either write or you don't. Nothing I can say is going to make you sit down and write. You have to want to do it. There are times when I don't want to do it. I'd rather go out and drink with friends, or hang out and watch sports and belch. But I don't. I write because I choose to. And that works for me.

2. Put your butt in the chair! Talking about your great script idea is not going to get it written. You can sit in all of the coffee shops and cafes you want and tell everyone about your movie, but until you sit down and write it, your idea doesn't mean squat. You're a poser.

If you want to join a writing group, go ahead. But check it out first, and make sure that other people in the group are as serious as you. Writing groups can be good places for feedback, but to get good feedback you have to write something.

Writing groups work best if you're doing the writing anyway, and there are members of the group whose opinions you respect. If you don't respect them and think they're full of shit, then what are you doing there?

Angry Filmmaker's note: I don't understand writing groups. A writing group can't make you write. I've seen writing groups where half the people rarely write anything. But they can sure tell you what's wrong with your script. If you're thinking on Tuesday night, that damn it, you have to crank out some pages before the group tomorrow night, and it feels like an obligation, then you're not ready to write.

I have a group of people who I have read my scripts for feedback. Most of them are not filmmakers or screenwriters. They are fiction writers, artists, friends, and, most important, people who are honest with me. If something isn't working, or they don't fully understand something, they tell me. They don't say, "This sucks! I hate it!"

They ask me lots of questions. "Why is this character doing this? It doesn't really make sense to me. What are you going for here?" Good honest questions about your work can take you a lot farther than just plain criticism. If enough people are having similar problems in a certain area of your script, or with your script in general, then you need to take a look at it and see what you're doing wrong.

Always have people you *trust* and *respect* read your stuff. In my opinion, the worst people to read your scripts are other filmmakers. Other filmmakers are extremely opinionated. They also get hung up on all sorts of minor details that most audiences never see or get. Or, they'll talk about a part in your script that is similar to something they saw on a Star Trek episode, or some obscure horror film. "Are you ripping them off? Or is it just an influence?" Who the fuck cares! Read and comment on MY script. Don't dump all of your own crap on me! The odds are I didn't see whatever obscure piece of shit you're talking about. I've been making movies, not watching them!

There is also a competitiveness among filmmakers. We say we want to help our friends, but how many of us want our friends to do better than us? Not many.

So when you're looking for feedback on a script, a rough cut, or whatever, make sure the people you're giving your stuff to don't have their own agenda. Make sure that anything they say is about you and your project, not about them.

The Internet: Not just for porn anymore

There are Web sites popping up all over where you can post your work and get feedback. But who are these other people? And what the hell are they doing giving feedback to total strangers? Don't they have lives? Probably not. Actually, many people in the film business don't have lives. If you think we're bad, wait until you check out true film geeks. Now, those people are scary, and did I say pathetic? Anyone who memorizes *Stars Wars* dialog, *Star Trek* episodes, or Cameron Diaz's bra size frightens me.

That's not to say all Web sites for feedback are bad. The Zoetrope Web site seems to be pretty good. You can also post short stories and novels in addition to screenplays. The thing that makes this one different is if you want people to read your work, you have to read theirs. You have to read a certain amount of other people's stories or screenplays before you can post and get feedback on your own. You have to join this one.

A friend of mine swears by the Zoetrope site for his short fiction. He and a few other people have become regular sounding boards for each other. They review each other and encourage each other. Now that's good.

He was going to submit a screenplay, but he knew he had to read a certain amount of other people's work before he could do that. He read four screenplays before he became hopelessly depressed and couldn't read any more.

Apparently, there's a lot of bad shit out there. Maybe that's where Francis gets his ideas. No, even he probably couldn't plow through all of the crap on his own site to find the few ideas that might be worth stealing. Maybe he keeps grabbing the wrong ones. Now, there's a theory.

There are also sites where you can post your screenplays, and people read them and vote for the ones they like best. And if you're lucky, then someone might option your screenplay, and maybe, just maybe, it might get produced.

VOTE on people's scripts! That's a great idea! I am sure that Picasso would sit around in his studio, do a bunch of drawings and then have people vote on which drawings they like the best, and those are the ones that he would paint. I can see Michelangelo letting people vote on what statue he should sculpt. "Should I do David? Or maybe King Solomon? Judas? Check out my ideas for Goliath. What do you guys like best?"

Angry Filmmaker's note: Writing (and filmmaking) should be about passion! You write a script because you need to. You have to! You need to get this stuff out of your system. I don't believe you write something because you know that it has been tested and it will appeal to a certain group. I know, I am in a minority here. But if you're going to go to all the trouble to create a story, write it, and rewrite it, again and again, then you should be passionate about it! Don't do it because of a fucking marketing survey!

So, you can post stuff on the Internet, but if you're worried about someone stealing your brilliant ideas, then don't post it. If I were you, I'd send your scripts straight to Hollywood studios, production companies, and agents. That way you are assured that your ideas are being stolen by professionals.

Okay, where were we? Oh yeah...

Finally, 3. PUT YOUR BUTT IN THE CHAIR! Are you sensing a pattern here? You have to do the work! No one is going to write it for you, (unless you're rich, and in that case, you probably have someone else reading this book for you as well). If you don't sit down, you're not going to end up with a script.

Now, this is where I love to drive students crazy. This is where I tell them to stop wasting time watching movies. Forget about movies. They're not going to help you with writing, unless, of course, you're going to write a script about making a movie, or a script that's a movie spoof, or a script with some sort of arcane film trivia in it.

If you want to do that, please put this book back on the shelf, and slowly back away from it. Leave the store and don't buy it! I will not be held responsible for spoofs, or movies about movies. They are usually stupid and an insult to most viewer's intelligence. Most of the good spoofs have already been done. If you still want to write something like that, I've got nothing to tell you. Books! That's what I'm afraid you're going to have to start reading. That's right, books. They're not evil, and they won't bite. They can actually teach you something. Like storytelling. Storytelling, what a concept.

Angry Filmmaker's note: What's the deal with these people who seem to be proud that they don't read books? What the fuck is up with that? You are proud of being an illiterate moron? Don't you people realize you learn from books? And if you don't like learning, books can also entertain? Sure you have to work at it, but books are something to be treasured and read. I just don't get people who don't like to read. I must be a snob.

Anyway, you might discover all sorts of amazing things out there in the world of books. Did you know that people make movies from books? Yes, they do. Some of them become really good movies. When you think of really good movies, what usually springs to your mind first? The story. Everything springs from the story.

Most of the writers I know are also readers.

You can and should read scripts. There are some Web sites and places you can go to and read old screenplays. If you are going to read other screenplays, then you should read screenplays of classic movies.

There are reasons these movies are classics. See what some of the great writers do with these scripts. Read *Chinatown, Sunset Blvd., Citizen Kane* (which is an over-rated movie, but we'll talk about that later), anything by Billy Wilder, or Dalton Trumbo. These people were masters of the craft. These are the people you can learn from.

Then go out and rent the movies that they wrote. See what the director did with their scripts. Remember, just about everything you see in a movie was on the page first. And here's an interesting thought: Do you think that these screenwriters watched a lot of movies on DVD and figured out how to tell stories from there? I don't think so. My guess is, they read books.

Remember, it's all about story. When you read a book, try to break down the story. Figure out how the author broke it down. A well written story is the basis for so many forms of art. All the great writers mastered the art of storytelling first. Then they moved around in different mediums: playwriting, novels, short fiction, screenplays. The good ones have one thing in common: GOOD STORIES! Interesting characters help.

I know I told you not to watch movies, and I guess I should amend that a bit. You should watch some of the classic films. And no, *Titanic* is not a classic. It just made a lot of money. Make watching good movies a habit. Watch films like ***Touch of Evil, Psycho*** (the original), ***To Kill A Mocking Bird, The Maltese Falcon, The Treasure of The Sierra Madre, Some Like It Hot,*** and see what made these films so good. What was it that you and others like about them? Those are the films you can learn something from.

You can watch other films, newer stuff, just don't become obsessed by them. Especially the science fiction ones, or anything by Spielberg. You can do better.

Blade Runner is an amazing film from a visual standpoint, but it really sucks when it comes to the story! I love watching it, then I feel like I've had too many Twinkies, and now I want some meat and vegetables. You are not going to get substance from movies like that. Why? It's the story, stupid!

So you've done a couple of drafts of your story and you've

handed out your script to a few people that you trust.

They need to read the whole script in one sitting.

A script should read like the movie would play. Each page is roughly one minute of screen time, and a feature length script should be 90 - 120 pages, give or take. Everyone writes differently, so we won't be sticklers here. It should take one of your confidants 90 - 120 minutes to read the thing, right?

If they're not willing, or can't read it in one sitting, then you don't have to take anything they say seriously. I mean, come on, is a theater going to let you come in, watch the movie for an hour, then let you go run some errands and come back to the theater for the last hour on the same ticket? I think not. Your friends need to sit down and read it all the way through in a single sitting. If they can't do that, it's either a really bad script, or your friends went to public school (they could have ADD, but I'm not a doctor or a health insurance underwriter, so I can't say).

Why do I insist that it has to be read in a single sitting? Because it has to flow, just like the finished film. Pure and simple.

Feedback Is Not Just for Guitarists

What do you look for when it comes to feedback?

Are the characters consistent? Do they make sense? Are there any glaring errors in logic? Are these characters you'd like to spend 2 hours with? Is the story interesting? Does it make sense? Did everything you set up in the beginning pan out in the end? Are there loose threads? Do characters appear and/or disappear for no apparent reason?

What you don't want are responses like, "I liked it." "It was good." "It's a nice little script." "Cool, I can't believe you did it." "How are you gonna do this?" "It sucked!" "I don't want to talk about it." "You are really messed up." or "You offended me!" (Actually, I do like this one.)

GET IT IN WRITING

If you can get people to write down their comments, all the better. Then you have something concrete you can deal with.

I give out short questionnaires with the scripts, including specific things that I am concerned about. That way, when people are done reading, they can answer questions. You get more specific feedback when you outline what it is you are looking for.

Start going through all your comments and look for consistency. Are there areas that people agree are problematic? Are there characters or situations that are unbelievable? Where is it that people agree? What are the things they like? You need to sift through all the feedback and see where the problems are. Then decide what's fixable and what isn't.

There are times that something is going to bother your readers, and if that's what you want, then it's time to say, "Most people don't like this part. Cool!"

In my mind, it's about consistency within the world that is the screenplay. That doesn't mean everything has to make sense in real life, it just has to make sense within the confines of the universe you created. One of my favorite books is *100 Years of Solitude* by Gabriel Garcia Marquez. Amazing things happen in this book that you believe. There are fantastic things that couldn't happen in real life. But Marquez has set you up from the beginning. He's taken you into his world, a world absolutely

43

consistent in its own way. You believe the most amazing things because he has set you up to believe them. I don't want to give away much about the book. Read it, and you will know what I mean.

Let's Put Our Butts in the Chair Again

It's time for another rewrite. Trust me, scriptwriting is all about rewriting. On all of my films, the rewriting never stops. On *Kicking Bird*, a week into the shoot, I realized that my ending was wrong. It didn't make sense. There was a major flaw (I'm not gonna tell you what it was), and I had to fix it while we were shooting. I didn't see the problem in the read-through with the cast, the rehearsals, or anywhere. No one else saw it either.

I was shooting one of the last scenes with Digger when I saw the problem. Luckily, I had a week before I needed to shoot the final scene, so I had time to rewrite. I didn't say anything to the cast. I just shot all day and went home every night and reworked the scene. When it was ready, I told everyone what the new ending was, and why. I think the ending is correct now. I'm just glad I found the problem before I shot it.

In *Birddog*, I wasn't so lucky. I had to make some changes on that ending. Originally, I had Harv writing a book based on the experience he just went through. He was a writer who was having a rough time with his career. He was lost, and he got screwed over. What better way to exact his revenge than to write a huge best-seller and get back at those who screwed him over. WRONG! It read like a lame ass movie of the week. It was bad TV. What was I thinking? That scene is in an original draft of the script, but it was never shot. I'm happy to say that I came to my senses before that happened.

The real problem, discovered in editing, was the final

confrontation between Harv and Ron. It fell flat in the editing room. It had no power, no punch. It read well in the script. It seemed to play well when we shot it, but once it was edited, it fell flat. I was exhausted and couldn't figure it out. So I brought a buddy of mine up from LA. Harry B. Miller III is the best editor I know. We've known each other since film school. Give him an editorial challenge and he's all over it. He graciously gave me two weeks of his time in between jobs. His first rule was that I was not allowed into the editing room while he was working, unless he invited me. That's a tough rule; he's in there with my child. But you have to let go and trust your editor.

I was locked out for a week, and then I came in for a screening. Another rule was that I wasn't allowed to say anything until the entire cut was over. I could take notes, but that's it.

When we hit the final confrontation, the scene started the same, but then it turned abruptly. As I started to jump out of my seat to yell, "Stop everything! What have you done?" Harry put his hand on my knee and quietly said, "Just watch." He had moved the head of the scene to the end, and started it with the ending.

It was perfect.

I had all the parts there, I just had them in the wrong order. *Birddog* starts off as a film about friendship between two characters, and then the specter of the Vanport flood comes into the picture. As I was working on the film, the flood seemed to take over the movie. The final confrontation scene started with their friendship and ended on the flood. Harry saw that the scene and the movie still needed to be about friendship. And that's how he cut it. As much as I'd like to say the brilliant work in the film was all mine, without Harry the film would not be as good as it is. Even in the editing room you have to rewrite.

Okay, you've got a script written, you've taken all of your

friend's comments and made changes and you think it's pretty brilliant. Now what? Well, you have a couple of choices here. You can register it with the Writers Guild to give yourself that false sense of security that your work of art is protected and no one can steal it from you.

You can run around LA and New York submitting it to various production companies and/or studios, or you can just make the damn thing yourself.

Angry Filmmaker's note: Anyone can and will steal from you. There's usually not a damn thing you can do about it, whether you register it or not. Ask Art Buchwald about *Coming to America* with Eddie Murphy. And remember, Art is a lot more famous than you are. (Actually, Art isn't writing anymore, talk to his estate.)

"I'll take Hollywood for $200, Alex"

So let's say you decide to play the Hollywood game. Here's what you're in for. Every year there are probably 15,000 scripts registered with the Writers Guild. How many movies do you think are actually made from those 15,000 scripts?

When you start sending your script around, you're probably going to get form letter rejections because you don't have an agent. How do you get an agent? God only knows. If you don't have an agent, any production company that is actually interested in reading your script is going to make you sign a blanket release. One that says you can't sue them if they end up making a "similar" movie they probably had in development long before you came along. Yeah, right.

Your script is going to be read by some kid fresh out of film school, or by some impressive Ivy League school guy who thinks it's fun to be in the film business as long as his/her trust fund holds out. This person goes home every night and writes their own script. He can't figure out why his work isn't selling and is pissed that after four years of college he's working for someone dumber than he is, and reading shit from idiots like you. Oh yeah, and they're not getting paid much, either.

Remember, the film business is glamorous and everyone wants to work in it. There are at least 20 people with graduate film degrees, hustling for every entry-level job, and foolishly thinking they can work their way up.

Of course they're not going to like your script! They'll send you that form letter saying thanks, but no thanks. Then they're gonna sit down and write their own stuff, and if some of your ideas pop up in their work... Remember, you signed the damn release.

But let's say you get past that, and you actually get a personal phone call. Hey, it happens! The development person really likes your script, and they think it could be good for Madonna/Beyonce/Kate/Ben/Tom. But they want to suggest some changes, and if you're willing to do a rewrite for FREE... Then IF it's good enough, MAYBE they'll show it to (fill in your own blank here). But you have to do the REWRITE FOR FREE.

Don't Pull Out That Champagne Just Yet

"This is fucking great," you say. "Of course I'll do it!" Guess what? You've fallen for it. You're going to do half a dozen rewrites, and your favorite actor will probably never see your script. After six months to a year of rewrites, their interest will fade.

Angry Filmmaker's note: Important Law in the Hollywood Film Business: No one ever gets fired for saying, "NO!" You only get fired for saying, "Yes" and costing the company money. As the legend goes, Verna Fields at Universal turned down George Lucas's script for *Star Wars* and was eventually promoted. Her comment: "If you had seen the version of the script that I saw, you would've turned it down, too." What a great cop-out! She is assuming that no one over at Fox read it before they green-lighted it. Actually, they probably didn't; they read "coverage," otherwise known as a one page treatment.

The other thing that you have to remember is nepotism. There are people who can get movies made in Hollywood because of who their parents are. You don't believe me? Look at some credits sometime. You don't think being Sofia Coppola helped get her movie made? It certainly wasn't her acting in *Godfather III*. And how many damn Coppolas are there in the business these days anyway? They are called Cage, Schwartzman, Shire, you name it!

There is also Jennifer Lynch, Jason Reitman, Danny Huston, Jake and Jon Kasden. I could go on forever. But I won't. And these are just director's kids. What about Gwyneth Paltrow, or Kate Hudson, or - - I am starting to get pissed here.

Making movies can be a family business. If your family isn't already in the business, it's going to be a lot tougher. I was visiting my alma mater (USC Cinema) a few years ago, and after touring the place, it seemed like a whole different world to me. When I was there, the school was full of outsiders, people who didn't fit in anywhere else. People were artists, or at least trying to be. Now the school looks like a giant fraternity/sorority party. I know there were outsiders somewhere, I just didn't see any. I was asking one of my old professors if they ever let the "riff-raff" into the program any more. The people who don't fit in?

He said, sadly, "No." A lot of the people in the program now were the kids of Hollywood people. It's no longer the way it was when I was there. No craziness, no breaking rules, or at least bending them (like Kevin Reynolds and his crew crashing a plane in the patio of the Cinema department to publicize his upcoming student film). My professor also felt, off the record, that the creativity wasn't there any more. Many of these students were only interested in making a film for their portfolio so that they could get a good job in the business. It was all about getting jobs, not about filmmaking!

I know from experience in this business, if you have to choose between two people to hire on your movie, are you going to choose a qualified stranger, or a less qualified buddy? We all know the answer to this one.

So the odds are that the Hollywood game isn't going to work out for you.

Hitting the Screenplay Lottery

You can enter your script in one of the many contests that are turning up all over the place. It is possible that you could win and have a studio make your script. It happened to Mike Rich with *Finding Forrester*. He has since gone on to write a bunch of scripts for Disney and is making quite a nice living. But Mike is the exception, not the rule. He's a talented guy who got lucky.

Think of all the people who've entered those contests for years and got nothing. You have as much of a chance of winning one of those contests and having your movie made as I do having monkeys fly out my butt!

Your only choice is to make the damn thing yourself. So let's get started...

CHAPTER 3:

Budgeting, or What Is It You REALLY Need?

"I think about budgeting during the writing stages. I think about budgeting during the thinking stages. I think about budgeting all the time."

I need to know how much money I think I can put together from the beginning. If I'm going to write something that's really expensive, then the script is going to sit in my file cabinet until Hell freezes over, Hollywood starts making good movies, or the studios start welcoming real independents with open arms. And we know the odds against any of this.

There are all sorts of software programs you can use to figure out your budget. They do the adding and multiplying, telling you how many crew people to hire, what you need to include for P&W (Pension and Welfare), painters, props and air transportation.

Forget that crap at this point. These software programs are not going to tell you what you really need. You still have to figure some things out for yourself. Before you waste your hard earned cash on a software program and start plugging numbers in, let's do some thinking.

ACTORS - Carbon-Based Props That We Really Need

Do you want to use a name actor for the lead? If so, start adding more money from the top. If you want William H. Macy, Alec Baldwin, or Kevin Spacey, it's gonna cost you some big dollars. If you want a really big "indie" star like Parker Posey, you're in luck. She's probably not as expensive.

Stars are commodities. If you have the money to pay a star yourself, maybe you should invest that money instead. It's a lot less risky than making a movie.

If you want to use a star of any sort, start adding figures for first-class travel and NICE hotels. Yes, I know it seems strange, but most of these people are not going to be interested in crashing on your couch, or taking your spare bedroom. They want their own place. If you're lucky, it's a couple hundred dollars a night for 4 weeks. Don't forget about their per diem and any other expenses they have, like an assistant, someone to watch their kids, someone to drive them around (okay, you can use a cheap production assistant for this one, but no PA should ever have to watch kids.) Are they going to need their own makeup people? Hairstylist?

Even a mid-level "star" is going to cost you, so think about that. If you have more than one name actor that you want, you're screwed. Stars and their agents can get into pissing matches with each other, and you might find you're making concessions to please one actor that totally pisses off the other. So it's back to the negotiating table, and that's gonna cost more money.

You want my advice? (You bought the book, so you must.) Avoid the star bullshit. There are plenty of great actors around who will work their asses off and give you great performances. They don't have big egos… yet.

The studio/distribution people will tell you that you need a name. Don't believe them. They're lazy. They don't want to have to work at their jobs. We work our asses off making the movie, why shouldn't they do the same thing promoting it? And these days, to say you have William H. Macy in a movie isn't enough. How many straight-to-DVD movies have you seen on the shelves that have name stars? If there are lots of titles that you have never heard of, just think how many movies these "stars" have done that never got picked up for the straight-to-DVD route. Probably lots.

It's all bullshit! Good actors are more important than stars any day of the week. Remember, stars have to come from somewhere. Maybe your low-budget film will be the launching point for the next Parker Posey? Doubtful, but possible. I still say, stay away from "stars!"

FILM/VIDEO STOCK AND CAMERAS - Film runs how fast?

You need to decide early on what you want to shoot. 35mm? Super 16mm? Regular 16mm? DV? Hi-Def?

The Macho Stock

35mm film looks best. It's the standard we're all used to. When your movie hits the big screen you want that 35mm look. When you're shooting, you want all that cool-looking 35mm gear that goes with this decision. You want the 5-and 10-ton trucks, the big lights, the army of gaffers and grips putting up lights and tearing them down, miles of stingers (extension cords) and the hum of the generator powering all of this stuff.

Now honestly, if you can afford all of this, why the hell are you reading THIS BOOK?

Okay, let's say we want to shoot 35mm. How can we cut down

some of our costs? (A lot of these tricks will apply to the other formats as well). What kind of film do you want to shoot? It is usually a choice between Kodak and Fuji.

Does your story take place mostly during the day or at night? What kind of look do you want? That full-on, beautiful, every-frame-is-a-portrait-that-can-be-hung-in-a-gallery-look? Or the gritty, washed-out look of urban America?

In my opinion, Kodak does the portrait stuff very well. If you run the lower speed stocks and can pump a lot of light through it, then it can look beautiful. I love Fuji because of its ability to look washed out. Most of my films are about working-class, down-on-their-luck, no future, kind of people. I like the washed-out look. Fuji can look pretty too; it always depends on what kind of light you're using and how much.

The important thing is, what is the look that's important to your story? Then call up representatives (salespeople) from both companies. Never go by their price lists! Tell them that you're going to be shooting a feature and that you want the best deal that they can give you.

They might want to know what groups you belong to, some, like the Independent Feature Project are good because Kodak will give you a 10% discount right off the top. The "student discount" thing works well too, but you have to prove that you are a student. These companies may be big, but they're not stupid.

My experience is that Kodak doesn't usually want to give you much of a deal beyond the 10 percent. They can be of the "take it or leave it school", because "we're Kodak." I think it's happening less and less because Fuji has made great in-roads with independents. So go to Kodak first, tell them how much film you need, and ask for their best price. Then take that price to Fuji. They'll beat it.

Now, you can play this one for a while if you want and get people to whittle it down further and further, but you're really not going to save all that much after the first go round. Also, these people are going to be wise to what you're doing, and maybe they'll say, "To hell with you. Go deal with the other guy."

Another source of cheap film stock used to be Studio Film & Tape Exchange in LA. (I can't find them on the Internet, I am not sure if they are still around.) There are other places like Media Distributors. They have what is called "re-can" stock, or "short ends." It's film that someone else bought new. It didn't end up getting used on the shoot, so they sold it to a company that specializes in selling this type of film stock. The stock is probably fine, but there is a danger.

You don't know how the other filmmakers stored the film stock. Were they making a film out in the desert? Did any of this film get up to 140 degrees? (That's bad.) Or were they doing a rafting movie and all of the stuff got dunked in a very cold river? (Also bad.) Or maybe this was that footage that's been sitting in the hot trunk of someone's car for awhile. (Not good.)

These places cannot, and will not, guarantee the stock. Yes, you can get insurance for faulty film stock, but it's only for new stock. Remember, it's an insurance company. Do you really think they're going to pay you? That's not how the insurance business works. You pay them. They screw you! Didn't you watch *Stolen Toyota*?

Angry Filmmaker's note: I have shot film from Studio Film & Tape Exchange and it was great! No problems, no anything. And the people there were great! I saved a good chunk of money and it all worked out. I hope they are still around.

I spent about $28,000 on 35 mm film stock for my feature, *Birddog*. That wasn't processing, printing, or even transfers. That was just buying the raw stock. And we got great deals. I also had a very low shooting ratio, around 7:1. For everyone foot of film used in the final film, I shot seven feet of raw stock. If my finished film was 10,000 feet in length, I shot a total of 70,000 feet.

Many of these Hollywood movies will shoot 100,000 feet of film just on second unit photography. Second unit photography can be shots of a city, characters driving from a distance, parking, or walking shots. It is usually a second unit shot if the main actors are not in it, or they can use a double (someone who physically resembles the actor from a distance) to get the shot they need. Why waste your actor's valuable time and skills if it is just a wide shot of them driving down the freeway. That's not what you're paying them for. Is it?

Not So Macho

Let's say you want to shoot Super 16mm because it's cheaper than 35mm. If it's lit right, it can look great. It is called Super 16 because the frame size is actually larger then regular 16mm. They only put sprocket holes on one side of the negative, so they can make a larger frame on the same size film stock. If I have to explain it more than that, go to film school.

If you're going to shoot Super 16, that means you probably want to blow it up to 35mm when you're all done and the negative is cut. Shooting Super 16 can save you a lot of money up front: the stock is cheaper, the camera rental is cheaper, and some people say that you can use less light, so the lighting is cheaper.

That last part is not necessarily true. In my opinion, if you are going to blow Super 16 up, then you need more light so that your eventual 35mm negative will look good.

I recommend shooting everything at least at an F5.6, if not an F8. You want a very thick negative, one with lots of latitude. If you shoot down around F2 and F2.8, your negative will be grainy and your blowup will be really grainy. Think about the look of the sand storm sequence in *Laurence of Arabia*. If that's the look you want, then go for it. Remember, you do need to rent a 16mm camera that will shoot Super 16 (you need a larger aperture). You will also have to have your film transferred to video, as there are not many super 16mm projectors around. Super 16 is truly intended for blowup or to finish in tape.

There's really no reason to shoot regular 16mm for a feature, so let's not even go there. You can do it. People have done it. Why?

It's Tape Time

If you really want to work cheap, then let's talk video. The only two real formats right now are HD (High Definition) and Mini DV. Betacam is being/has been phased out.

Angry Filmmaker's note: Here's a side bar to all of you video manufacturers out there. How about some fucking standards!!! Sony goes one way, first with Beta Max vs VHS, then they have DV cam which is not compatible with anyone but themselves. Their 24p isn't really a true 24p, and now they have their own version of HD.

You know, I can grab any film camera anytime and throw a roll of film into it, and it's gonna run at 24 frames a second (25 if I'm in Europe). I can play a print back on any damn projector I can find. But not with video! I need Sony stuff if I want to shoot DV cam, plus there's 24p to transfer better to film. Would you guys just sit down at a table like the SMPTE (Society of Motion Picture and Television Engineers) guys did years ago? Come up with some damn standards because I'm really getting pissed off here! Oh, and by the way, video guys, FILM STILL LOOKS BETTER!

So anyway... HD. It looks good, and with this new generation of small HD cameras, there is almost no reason not to shoot it. You do have to have HD editing programs, but it's getting to be the standard. TV will be broadcasting nothing but HD, so definitely take all this into account. And remember, by the time this damn book is published, probably all of this will have changed.

Why can't we all just shoot Mini DV? If you light it like you're lighting film, it can look great. There are tons of good mini DV cameras that can be had for free or very cheap. Everyone who went out and bought mini DV cameras early on are now trying to get rid of them so they can buy HD cameras. Remember this. These people are probably willing to make a deal.

What kind of a look are you going for? If it's scratchy and hand held, then with DV, you're set. You might not even have to light!

Mini DV is inexpensive, it's easy to come by and can look good.

If you have money, shoot film. If you have less money, shoot HD. If you have no money, shoot mini DV.

LOCATION SOUND - Never hire a guy with hearing aids

No matter what camera system you use, you need to figure out sound. You should always hire an EXPERIENCED LOCATION SOUND RECORDIST. Don't worry, I'll repeat this one over and over.

Remember, a film can look like shit, and people will think it's arty. Look at the **Blair Witch Project** or the Dogma film, **The Celebration.** They both look like crap. One was a huge award-winner and the other made lots of money. The thing about both of those movies, is you can hear and understand all of the dialog. If your dialog sounds like shit, people won't watch it. Badly recorded dialog is what we like to call torture. Don't ever forget this!

Whether you're shooting film or video, you should have some kind of a digital recorder, a Hard Drive recorder, a time code DAT or even a time code Nagra. Don't record on to the video if you can avoid it. Video cameras are built to give you a good image, and the sound heads are okay, but recording sound with a good microphone on a separate machine is always better. It's a quality thing. You should really try to hire a separate boom operator. It'll make your sound that much better.

Good sound recordists come with their own gear and should cut you a deal, depending on how many days you're shooting.

COSTUMING - How many pairs of shoes do we need?

Is your movie a period piece? Science fiction? Didn't I warn you earlier about writing for your budget? What about costuming? I have the greatest costumer (Mary Chris Mass). She shops at thrift stores, she borrows, and she scams. She knows what I want and always works within my budget.

If your lead actors are going to be dressed in the latest fashions, unless they own those clothes anyway, it's going to cost you. There is the old "buy and return" scam. Buy a piece of clothing, use it in a scene, then try and return it to the store to get your money back. Remember, you need to keep it extremely clean or they won't take it back. Oh yeah, and don't tell any of the clerks that you're making a movie in conversation. They'll figure out what you're doing and won't take the clothes back. They're not that dumb.

If you can have cast members wear their own clothes, it's going to be cheaper, but who's going to be in charge of making sure they bring the stuff to the set everyday? And what happens if something rips?

In *Kicking Bird,* I wrote about two white-trash high school kids and I had them wear the same outfits everyday. It's believable for their characters, and it was always easy to remember what clothes they needed. Even with that, one guy would still forget things.

In *The Gas Cafe,* the story takes place over a few hours, so all the actors wore the same clothes for the entire movie. The wardrobe impact on the budget was minimal. Once again, one actor was always forgetting something. Try not to let the actors take their wardrobe home. That can only cause problems. In my movies, wardrobe is not a huge cost.

Really think about what your cast should be wearing.

SET DESIGN - Yes, we put that there

You're going to need a set designer/art director and a couple of props people. Don't forget props, unless of course you're making a Dogma movie. (In Dogma films, props can come from no farther away than 25 yards from the location).

You need to make sure in your script breakdown that you break out what props you're going to need for what scene, and someone has to be responsible for having them there.

Nice people will loan you props. Not so nice people will make you pay for them.

There are some people who won't loan you the stuff you want, like that Ferrari over there, or the giant inflatable Godzilla. You're going to have to buy stuff. Once again, what's your film about, and what's important? A buddy of mine bought some really weird science fiction costumes from some guy and then wrote a script around the damn costumes! Strange but true.

Get a set designer/art director who can do things on the cheap. And try to use existing stuff as much as possible. It's easier and faster.

Now go out and buy that fancy budgeting program. There are a few out there, and they're pretty good to have. Some software packages include script break-downs and help you put together your shooting schedule. It's really nice to just plug numbers in on various lines in the budget and let the program do all of the figuring for you.

Angry Filmmaker's note: When it comes to budgeting, remember, EVERYTHING IS NEGOTIABLE! Don't pay full price for anything! See what kind of deals you can work with cast and crew members. It's really important to pay your cast and crew a reasonable wage if you have money.

CREW - Your new best friends

If you have the budget, pay livable wages. If not, you owe your cast and crew, big time.

If you don't have money, you might want to have them sign an agreement that if your film makes money, they will get paid. These are called deferments. Usually, if someone asks you to defer payment on a movie, just kiss the cash goodbye. It's not going to happen. When I've had people defer on my films, I have every intention of trying to sell the movie and pay these deferments. The truth is I haven't been able to pay deferments. My movies get seen, but I haven't made enough money on any of them to start paying. I continue to try.

Now, if everyone who reads this book runs to my Website and starts buying my movies, then maybe I could do that. All of the distributors have let me down over the years. I'm still hoping that some of you out there won't.

Personally, I try to use my cast and crew on paying work whenever possible. They know if I can't pay them on one of my movies, they'll make it up with other paying work from me later.

Whether people are working for big bucks, or for free, treat them all the same -- with respect! We'll talk more about that later.

CRAFT SERVICES - A Well Fed Crew is a Happy Crew

What's the most important item in the budget?

FOOD, you moron! You need to feed people! You can get away with not paying them, but you need to feed them, and feed them well. None of this loaves of bread and peanut butter on the set. You need hot food, tons of water, coffee, tea, juices, snacks, and sugar. You need tons of food.

Angry Filmmaker's note: If you are doing the famous actor thing, figure that you're going to need a caterer and that's going to be in the thousands of dollars, because you have stars and other big-shots on your set, so everyone demands great (and expensive) food.

Never underestimate the power of hot, good food.

When we made *The Gas Cafe* for $4,000, the largest single budget item was food! These people are working their asses off for you, so if you want them to show up, feed them! A film crew, like the military, travels on its stomach. The better fed people are, the happier they are, the harder they'll work. If you need to shoot later than you planned, and you have treated the crew right and fed them well, they'll stay.

And sometimes you just have to buy the crew a beer. Although I'm probably not supposed to advocate that because of insurance issues. (Remember, if it were up to insurance people, no one would ever do shit because it's too dangerous, and we'd still have to pay our high premiums.) One or two beers will also buy you some loyalty, if it's good beer. If it's that Budweiser or Coors crap, forget it, your crew is either gonna be sick the next day, or they're not coming back. Buy good stuff. Just remember, do it on occasion, not all the time.

PUBLICITY - Just another person to get in your face about something

You're supposed to have a publicist, so you had better budget one. You know, someone who can have the local TV stations come out to your set, talk to you and act like this is a big Hollywood thing. They say you can use this footage as part of your "package" when you're trying to sell your movie. Personally, I've never seen anyone include something like this in a publicity package.

And don't forget, if you're shooting in your hometown, you need to talk about how much you like it, and how you would never, ever move to LA or New York. Your hometown is probably pretty good, and you might even be a celebrity there, but we all know you're lying. You think your hometown is holding you back, and you can hardly wait to make your blockbuster, move to LA, and never see the place again, except for when you're grand marshal of some fucking parade.

Good luck. If you escape, you're probably doomed to be a PA in LA, working for some idiot you're smarter than.

Anyway, you are supposed to budget for tons of publicity stills, which should require an expensive photographer and not one of your friends. You'll need to budget money on glossy publicity packets, and let's make sure we're shooting a behind-the-scenes documentary about your movie because no one's ever done that before.

You know something, you're going to be budgeting for all sorts of stuff that really has nothing to do with making your movie. This stuff is supposed to be for promoting your movie once it's done, if you get the money.

I do believe that you need good images to promote your movie, just don't go overboard.

Remember, if you can raise it, someone on your crew can spend it.

Angry Filmmaker's note: Personally, I don't give a shit if the local yahoos come to my set. I'm working. I do have friends show up and do stills on occasion, which does help. These friends are experienced photographers.

Hire a publicist? You have got to be fucking kidding me! I'm making a movie here. I also tried that "behind-the-scenes documentary" crap once, and it drove me crazy. When we finally cut the footage together, I don't think anyone ever even looked at it. For me, it was a waste of time and a waste of energy. It is hard enough raising money, so you should spend it on something that is going to show up on the screen!

POST-PRODUCTION - Not so fast, we're not done here yet

Everyone always budgets pretty well for preproduction and production, but where they always fall short is in post-production. No one ever thinks about post! Like, once you get through production, the rest of the film will take care of itself.

The odds are that someone is going to go over budget somewhere in production and you're going to take the money out of the post budget.

What do you need to think about for post-production? What kind of an editing system are you going to use? Avid? Final Cut? A flatbed? (Yeah right, most of you probably don't even know what a flat bed is, let alone how to use it.)

If you shoot film, you're probably going to transfer it to tape. What's that gonna cost? Make a deal with your local film-to-tape transfer house.

DAILIES

The footage you shoot on location is referred to as "dailies." It's an old term. Crews usually get together at the end of the day and watch the footage they shot the previous day.

We had our dailies done twice a week, at night, and done as a "one light." "One light" means no color correction, the colorist figures out the best setting for the first scene on the roll, and everything is corrected the same way.

We were shooting in 35mm and I had planned on finishing in

film anyway. Sure, we couldn't watch dailies every night after the shoot like the big-shots do, but we didn't have the budget to reshoot anything, anyway.

We gave the transfer house a bunch of recycled Betacam tapes to put our dailies on. I wasn't going to waste my money buying new tapes that were only going to get used once.

In all of the years I worked for Gus Van Sant and others, the studios would send us brand new tapes for every dub of whatever it was you wanted and needed. I started saving all of those tapes and when the shows were over, I'd record over them. Studios always buy new stuff, so I knew that these tapes had only been used once. Tape stock is not cheap if you're buying it from someone besides the manufacturer, and I wasn't going to pay the mark-up! I'm a cheap bastard, damn it!

I easily saved a few hundred bucks by recycling tape stock I already had. And I saved even more money on having the transfer house only transfer our stuff twice a week.

EDITING - What's it going to take to put this monster together?

I cut my first feature, *Birddog*, on an editing system called the D-vision. Why? Because I owned it. It didn't cost me anything. If you have your own editing system, you can rent it back to the production and make a few bucks on the side. You probably won't do that, but if someone has raised the money and you're not getting much of a salary, then why not?

As much as people scoffed at my old D-vision, the negative cutting list it generated was almost perfect when we finished. An old out of date system, absolutely. No fancy bells and whistles. It just did what it was supposed to do and that was edit the movie and keep track of all the key codes. You can't ask for more.

How many weeks are you going to edit? Are you editing yourself? If you're going to hire someone, what kind of hours are they going to work? Is it a fifty hour week? Sixty? Do they get overtime? Do they need an assistant? Do you? On some features, there are two assistants, and sometimes two editors. It depends on your schedule and your bank account. How fast do you need to get the movie out?

If you have to rent a system, or an editing room, then you want a monthly rate, not daily or weekly. And if you are going to edit for ten weeks or more, then you should get a really cheap rate or a week or two for free.

Most Hollywood films, and many of the so called Indie features, shoot film, edit video and conform a film work print to their video cut. They use the conformed work print for screenings so they can see their picture on a big screen, and if your budget is large enough and you have a bunch of executives breathing down your neck they want to screen a film print in a screening room. They can't be expected to make decisions based on what they've seen on a video monitor. (Personally I think it's a penis thing, but that might just be me.)

Is this what you need to do? Is this what you want to do? You are going to have all of the costs of editing in film, plus the costs of editing video. You'll have both a flatbed editing machine for the film, and an Avid or Final Cut Pro system for the video transfers.

This sounds like overkill, and in my opinion, it is. But if you are working with "stars," you will probably be doing preview screenings as well. I'll talk about preview screenings when we get to the editing section.

MUSIC - I know a guy in a band

What about music? If you use existing music you're going to be paying a lot of money to a bunch of people. Why? Because the Beatles didn't write all of that music just for you NOT to pay them (or Michael Jackson) for using it in your movie.

There are always stories and rumors that say if you only use a certain amount of music, or if it's unrecognizable, you don't have to pay for it. WRONG! You pay for every moment you use. And music, like actors, gets more expensive the more well known it is. Sure, I know you love Springsteen, but don't use his tunes unless he says it's okay. And he has to say it in writing, not in one of your dreams.

You can budget for original music, and that works out well if you know some good composers. Believe me, everyone with a computer and a keyboard thinks they can compose music. You can also approach local bands who write their own stuff. They are more likely to license stuff to you for cheap because they want to get their music out there.

When I work with local musicians, my standard deal is that they own the copyrights to their work. I have permission to use it in my movie and for promoting it. I have non-exclusive rights. If they have the opportunity to sell it to someone else, they can, and I get nothing. It's their music! I'll talk more about this later.

SOUND EDITING - What do you mean there's nothing left in the budget

Shall we talk about sound editing? That's the thing that you're required to do after you decided that anyone can record location sound and hired a friend of a friend of yours to do it. Listen, if people have trouble understanding the dialog, as I said before, you're screwed! You are now going to have to spend lots of time fixing your sound instead of designing it.

I think you're going to need at least one dialog editor, a couple of people to cut sound effects. If you can afford foley, then you should hire two walkers and a studio that specializes in foley. This is going to cost you some money. Once again, the more experienced people you hire, the faster they're going to work and the better your sound is going to be. Why do you need foley? Check the chapter on Sound Design. I don't have time for this.

SOUND MIX - DON'T EVER CALL THIS SWEETENING!

Sweetening is what you do to ice tea! We don't put sugar on our audio, ever! We mix sound, we blend the various elements. More on this in the audio chapter. But if I ever hear you talk about sweetening, I am going to come over there and kick some...

Anyway, let's talk about budgeting a sound mix. I know what you're going to say, "We're just going to do it on a buddy's Pro-Tools in his basement. In fact that's where we're going to do all of our sound."

Good luck, dudes. It's going to sound great on someone else's system, and your DVDs will probably sound okay in the living room, but any place bigger than that, it's not going to sound good at all.

Why? Because big rooms and theaters have big sound systems and big acoustics. If your film is going to play in a theater, you want to mix it to sound best in a theater. Your living room is crammed with furniture, people talking, all sorts of stuff. But a theater, well, it's crammed with chairs and people talking, but it's supposed to sound better. The little mistakes that you made on the sound are going to sound HUGE in a big room. That's why you need to hear it that way while you're mixing. Once again, you're spending money.

How many different versions of the mix are you going to have to do? Dolby Digital? SDDS? DTS? Television? Foreign? DVD? There are so many types of mixes you are required to deliver to most distributors. Do you know what they are and how much extra time they'll take? Find a good experienced mix facility that can do what you need them to do. And make sure they have some experience! You don't want to be someone's first mix.

TITLES - Now come the arguments

What about titles? For fancy titles, you can hire someone. With all of the people who own Photoshop and After Effects, anyone can create the stuff, but can they do it well? If you go with established places, you're going to spend money but have great titles. And we all know that good title sequences are really what movies are all about.

I put very few titles at the beginning of my movies. Why? Because no one has ever heard of my cast or the crew. So let's just start the movie! There will be plenty of time later to read the credits.

NOW WHAT? - We've got to finish this thing

How are you going to master your movie? Are you cutting a negative? Are you mastering on video? How much do you need to allot for all of this?

If you are cutting a 35 mm negative, you should call your local film processing lab and find out who they would recommend to cut your negative. They will also have price lists on A Rolls, A&B Rolls, Answer Prints, Release Prints, Intermediates, and Optical Tracks. What about color correction?

There are a lot of steps to go through to get a final film print, and trust me, they aren't cheap! I have had good luck with CFI, Deluxe, and Fotokem in LA. They have always treated me really square.

If you are finishing digitally, what will be your final master? Tape? What kind of DVD master do you want? Are you going to finish everything in your editing system, or are you going to a full-on post house to master it all there? What about color correction? Do you have an Avid Mojo? Or are you doing it in Final Cut? Are you going to "up rez" to HD?

Find a good post house that can give you options and costs for all of this. Talk to them until you know all your options.

The people who run post houses know their business. Talk to them and get your best prices. Then talk to someone else and make sure their prices are in line with each other.

STICK A FORK IN IT - This budget is done

The upshot is this: If you think you can raise the money, then go for 35mm, get a couple of indie stars, spend money on publicity, the editing, the mixing, and yes, even the sound. You'll be very happy. Your budget will be in the $2-4 million dollar range and, by God, you'll be an "Indie Filmmaker," provided of course, you can raise that sort of money.

If I'm doing this, I'm calling in every favor I can and a lot of ones that I don't have. Here's how I budget:

MY BUDGETS - Making very little go a long way

I'm going to shoot Mini DV or small format HD because the cameras are cheaper. I have friends who own them. I hire the same people on my commercial jobs that I do on my movies, so I can probably borrow a camera. So far, no cash outlay except for tape stock, and I can buy 8 boxes of 30-minute tapes (20 hours) for a couple hundred bucks.

Screw famous "indie" actors! I'm going with good actors who I know, actors I've worked with before and like. There are a lot of actors that work hard and are very good. These are the ones that I want. I don't care what anyone says, when I watch many of today's actors, I am not impressed.

Angry Filmmaker's note: And why do all of these singers think they can act? They can barely sing. I have no patience for the interchangeable Simpson girls, most rappers, or too skinny, phony blond debutantes who end up in movies, for no apparent reason other than marketing. Remember how bad an actor Sting was? I care about performance. Make me believe! And if you are just there for marketing reasons, get the fuck out! Some people can pull this off, most can't!

I like unknowns because maybe they really are those characters. I think they can be more convincing than some established actors because we don't know what they sound and look like.

If I can pay the actors something, I do. If not, I make sure we all participate in any profits the movie might make (so far no luck yet, but I'm trying). A talented friend of mine helps me cast the other roles I haven't written for specific people. We tell everyone, up front, about the lack of cash and what is expected of them if they agree to work with us.

If some one turns us down because we have no money, I thank them for their time, and move on.

I get my locations any way I can. I ask for permission, I beg for permission, I come and shoot when no one's around. I hate permits! Permits are just a way for your hometown to figure out how to make money off of you without providing any real service.

Same with state film boards. If you're from out of state and have some money (not even lots), they'll bend over backwards for you. Try working with your own film commission without money or stars. They're always too busy. That's my experience in Oregon anyway. I no longer ask. I just do.

My casts and crew are usually pretty small, so we blend in. I have shot in public places on weekends and holidays because city offices are usually closed. And most law enforcement folks have better things to do than hassle you if you're not causing problems.

If I'm busted at a location, I apologize, feign ignorance and quietly leave. You've been busted. You know it. They know it. Why make a big deal out of it? Because you'll probably be back tomorrow.

The only exception to this "no permit" policy is if I have a scene with a gun in it! Then I do ask permission, get a permit, alert the police, the neighbors, anyone I can think of. There is nothing worse than having your shoot interrupted by a SWAT Team. You will get local publicity, but I wouldn't necessarily call it good local publicity. And you don't want anyone getting hurt.

If I use friends' places as locations (their businesses or homes), I always thank them with a restaurant gift certificate, or bottle of wine, whatever. It's not much, but it shows that I am sincerely appreciative to them for helping me. Which I truly am. I have used my house more often than I care to admit. It's free, and sooner or later I get it back to normal.

Locations should cost nothing.

I write my scripts so that lots of scenes occur outdoors. Why? Less lighting. We use reflectors or move people around to get good lighting. The setup times are faster, and that way I can usually borrow a light kit or two with some simple grip equipment. Even when I have to rent this stuff, I'm not renting much, so my costs are low. Then I negotiate down from there. If I can get a cost break, I will. I also own a lot of long extension cords! If I have to pull power from somewhere, I want lots of cable.

Since most of my characters are down on their luck, I use thrift shops or actor's personal wardrobes. In *Kicking Bird* the two main characters wear the same clothes for the entire movie. They're teenage boys and they're poor. Nothing fancy here, and I will bet that most people will never notice, or they accept it as part of their character. One less thing to worry about on the set.

I always shoot in the shitty month of January when no one's working and so people are available for a few days here and there. No big deal. I also hire some young people to help them get experience, never as department heads, but lots of assistants. The good ones learn fast and move up the ladder.

My location sound people are usually very experienced, as is my director of photography. I have used some younger, less experienced sound people and I will listen to playback on the set during the first few scenes, so I know that it sounds good. I always let them know if they have any problems, or think there might be, tell me. I'll either do it again for sound, or listen to it and determine if I need to redo it. Most sound people have their own gear, so I pay for tape and batteries.

Also if they are available, I try to wear Comteks (wireless headphones), that way I can hear everything that is going down on the tape. If there is a sound problem, I know about it right away and can do another take.

I usually give everyone gas money, depending on the locations. I give the makeup people money for supplies, and I have enough general supplies (slates, camera tape, gaffer's tape, etc.) to take care of most shoots. If I have to buy gels for lights, I will (but I have a bunch of old stuff left over). I've accumulated some lights over the years that still work fine. If I don't need to buy it, I won't. If I do need it, and it will save time on the set, then I'll always spend the money. If things go faster and smoother, that's money well spent.

I do spend money on food! I've been lucky finding caterers who are really good and can work wonders on very little money. I explain how many people I need to feed, and whether I want hot or cold (usually both). Good sandwiches are always an option. We make it work, and this is the one area I usually go over budget on. Oh well.

I do all of my snack shopping at places like Costco, and I use coupons at regular grocery stores and stock up on stuff that's on sale. I wish I could tell you that I only buy name brands, but I rarely do. If it's a local brand or the store's bargain brand, then that's what I'm going with. Most of the time it's fine. And if I do make a mistake with this stuff, I rectify it real fast. I work my ass off being organized (Chapter 5) so my cast and crew don't have much standing around time. We get more work done in a shorter period of time.

When it comes to post, I own my own editing system: an Avid Express DV Pro, which is better than owning a camera. It still works fine even if some geeks consider it obsolete. So my editing room costs me nothing. I spent years working professionally as an editor, so I do the feature work myself.

Since I have done sound design on so many other people's films, I have a bunch of sound editors as friends. I can usually con them into editing a reel or two for me for nothing in their spare time. I have arrangements at various mixing studios so I can usually get a really cheap rate to be deferred for my mix.

I can usually find a theater that will let me sneak in and play back my mix so I can hear how it sounds in a big room.

I do all my color correction either on Avid's Mojo (I have friends who own one and they cut me a killer deal), or I go into a large post house on a weekend or right after a holiday when they are closed. A lot of times if you slip an employee a few bucks, they'll come in and do it for you. It's great to have someone working with you who is learning the ropes. They work slower, but you are sitting with them so they can't mess it up too badly...

After 20 years in the business I have a lot of friends. I've done a lot of favors for others and hired a lot of people for various paying projects. I'm lucky that so many people help me, and I always make sure that they are aware of how much I appreciate it. That's why I can make films on a shoe string. It's one part philosophy, one part the help of others, and one part planning.

CHAPTER 4:

FINANCING or I don't have that kind of money!

"You have your budget together and now it's time to go out and raise some money. GOOD FUCKING LUCK!"

Sooner or later you're going to encounter someone who's going to tell you that they can raise money, and they want to work with you. "You know, it's a lot easier to raise 2 million dollars than it is to raise just a million." is what you're going to be told. I want you to look into that son of a bitch's eyes and calmly say to them, "Bring me back $10,000 and I might believe you!"

Angry Filmmaker's note: I don't know what it is, but I have heard that line so many fucking times by people who then go out and raise nothing! It's Bullshit! Raising money for movies is hard work. These people who raise money for other things and think they can do it for you are full of shit. They don't know. Investing in a movie is a bad investment! The only people who should do it are people who can afford to lose their investment! This business is not for the faint of heart, I don't care how much you think you know.

So now you have a $3 million budget and you have people telling you that they can raise the money, but first, you need a business plan. Well, that makes sense because that's how

businesses raise money. After 20-plus years in the business
I can tell you, as an independent filmmaker, this business is like
no other. It just isn't. We don't have regular income, regular
"receivables," depreciation, none of that.

When I first got into the business, my accountant gave me some
very prudent tax advice in November: "tell your clients not to
pay you until after the first of the year. Then take out a loan for
90 days and invest in equipment. Then after the first of the year,
you can pay off the loans with the money you're owed. Take the
tax deduction for the previous year, and you'll be in good
shape." It made sense to me and everyone else I talked to
because we all went to art school! I almost went bust because
of that advice!

Right after I bought all of that equipment, business dropped off
severely. The film business can be seasonal, especially if you
are outside of LA. In Portland, it usually dies off around
Thanksgiving and doesn't start picking up again until mid- to
late February. Sometimes it stays busy through the end of the
year, but don't count on it.

A lot of the corporate and commercial people who hire us need
to get things done and money spent before the end of their fiscal
year. Then they take the holidays off. Why not? They have
steady salaries. After the first of the year, they need to put
together budgets and plan for the rest of the year. This is a cycle
I have seen over and over. There have been exceptions to this,
but rarely.

By the time I got paid on what I was owed, I had other debts
that accumulated, and guess what, gang? Banks will not loan
you money when you need it! They only loan you money when
you have money. (Don't get me started here, I hate bankers.)

Anyway, I spent nine months in hell trying to pay my bills, and I had a bunch of equipment that suddenly felt like a burden.

The upshot of all of this is:

DON'T LISTEN TO BULLSHIT MONEY PEOPLE!

If you're going to do a business plan, that's going to take time and money. There are software programs that can do business plans for you, but I've never seen one that is for the film business. You have to use software based on traditional business practices, and try to make it work for a nontraditional business.

I mean, as filmmakers, how many of us really have "receivables?" Trying to figure out your monthly income is like catching water in a net. Some years I do great, some years my income sucks! Ask Uncle Sam.

Anyway, you're going to need a lawyer and probably all sorts of other people to help you write this thing.

Angry Filmmaker's note: How come your "money people" can't sell anything without a business plan, yet they can't write it themselves?

Depending on how you're looking for investors and what you're selling them, you might also have to register with the Securities and Exchange Commission, so prepare to spend more money and time doing paperwork for the government. Consult a lawyer.

Now there's a bunch of money going out to write something that isn't making your movie. "Don't worry" you're told. "Once I get this plan I can really sell this thing." Prepare to hear a variation of this line a lot.

Six Degrees of Kevin Bacon

Your "new" partner wants a couple big actors to include in the business plan. "It'll be a lot easier to sell to investors," they say. You might want to go after Kevin Costner, Jim Carrey, or Julia Roberts.

What you will end up with is some guy or girl who played the kid, or the best friend, in an obscure Kevin Bacon movie.

Anyway, you make a bunch of copies of your script (better make some copies of your synopsis as well; most people in the business don't like to read scripts - actually, most of them don't like to read at all).

Next, make some phone calls to SAG (Screen Actors Guild) to find out who the agents are for the actors you want for your script. Get the agents' names and phone numbers, call them, talk to an assistant, and maybe, you'll get permission to send your script to them.

They always ask, "By the way, who's funding this?" You say you're trying to raise money, but if their actor could just read the script, they could see that they are perfect and the film could really be a big hit for them.

You send scripts to agents. Some actors may read them and might give you a letter. But this may or may not help your fund-raising efforts. Many of these letters are extremely vague. Many actors are advised not to be too specific about a commitment. They saw what happened to Kim Basinger and *Boxing Helena*. If you don't know what happened, go to the Internet and look it up!

The letters you get will say that **IF** you can get funding, then they **MIGHT** be interested and available to be in your movie.

Some actors do this not just for your project, but others as well. Because who knows, maybe you will get the funding and actors are always looking for work and a decent payday.

Before you get your business plan done, you need to actually form a business. There are a ton of different ways to do this, depending on where you live, and what regulations your state has. Once again, it's going to cost you money.

There are a million questions about partnerships

You are going to need a lawyer and an accountant to help you with this one. Don't look at me. I've made enough of my own mistakes. I am not going to make any for you. **I am not a lawyer or an accountant!** Like I said, talk to someone who knows.

Angry Filmmaker's note: There is an old joke and I don't know who said it first. It applies to a lot of businesses, but I think it especially applies to this one. It goes: Do you know how to make a small fortune in the movie business? Start with a large one!

So you drop a bunch of money into the business plan, and from what I understand, it can cost up to $10,000 to properly do something like this. Now you have to go out and find the investors. Your business buddy is going to be meeting people for lunch, drinks and stuff like that. And who's going to pick up the tab on all of this?

Did you know you have to disclose to potential investors that, in all likelihood, they are never going to even get back their original money, let alone make anything on it? That's right. You have to tell them up front they are probably going to lose their entire investment. Maybe it's a tax write-off. Maybe not. Who knows? Especially the way the government keeps changing the rules on this stuff. Since it's harder to find investors, my guess is that it's not a write-off anymore.

The 1980"s were the glory days of tax loopholes and being able to invest in movies and deduct it all. But guess what? It isn't the '80s anymore. All of those loopholes, incentives, tax dodges, whatever you wish to call them, are gone. For most people, there is no longer an incentive to invest in movies. (If you ask Willie Nelson, there isn't a lot of incentive to invest in anything anymore, but that's a different story.)

Many states (and countries) are offering incentives to shoot in their towns and cities, but usually what the offer are tax breaks or rebates based on how much you are going to spend there. You can't (or at least shouldn't) count that as money in your budget, because it could all change before you finally shoot.

Sooner or later, people are going to ask to see your previous work. You are the writer/director, after all. Maybe you've made some short films, or directed some commercials, or corporate videos or something. So they look at that and say, "Have you ever directed a feature?" Now, if you have, you wouldn't have shown them the other work in the first place. You would have shown them the damn feature! But you don't have one.

This week, the media is telling us the hot thing in the film business is short films. All the hot young directors are making short films and that's what studios and movie companies want to see. Yes and no. Most of the shorts they're looking at are from film school kids. USC has a couple of big industry screenings a year to show off the work of their students. I'm sure other schools do this as well. Lots of lower level executives show up to these things. They don't want to be left out, or miss something. Oh yeah, and it's part of their job since they're on the lower end of the food chain at their office. Sometimes people will look at your short film, usually not.

A lot of film schools out there promote their students, their programs, and anything else they can think of with short films. Everybody is doing it. Will your student short get you a directing gig on a feature? Beats me.

To have real credibility, you need to have made something before, and it had better be good. If it looks amateurish and is nothing like the epic you want to make, then you're stuck. It's going to be tougher, but not impossible.

Angry Filmmaker's note: And just because you've made other films doesn't mean any of this is going to be easier. I find that it gets harder every time.

At some point your money raiser is going to talk about how sexy the movie business is, and that's why people want to invest in it. It's sexy if you're shooting in Paris, you have some big-name stars, and you know this film is going to go to the Cannes Film Festival, and you and your investors are going to be drinking champagne on the Miramax yacht, or the Weinstein Co. yacht, or whatever they're calling it this year.

But you're making a small independent movie with B-list actors, and you're hoping for Sundance in the middle of winter. Still, sort of sexy, but not quite. You're probably going to end up at some small film festival in New Jersey playing to a half-full room.

Your money raiser is going to do a bunch of meetings, and if you live in a modest-size city you're going to get trotted out to a bunch of these. You're going to meet all of these people, and the first one or two meetings are going to seem great. These people seem really interested.

Wrong. Unless they pull money out right on the spot, you're not going to get any. Always remember: yes means yes, but maybe means NO! It's just going to take you a while to get to NO!.

You'll hear about them discussing it with their lawyers, accountants, partners, wives, partner's wives, whatever. It all means the same thing: They're not going to say "No" right then, but they will later, after they've eaten and when they don't have to do it to your face.

Sooner or later, you will hear the bullshit line, "I know I'm going to regret this when you're standing on the stage receiving your Oscar, but I think I am going to pass." I hate that line! It is so phony and disingenuous. They aren't going to regret shit! Basically, they think you can't do it, but they're trying to stroke your ego. If you ever do get into a position of power or fame, they can say something lame like this to try to get back into your good graces. Did anyone notice USC falling all over itself, kissing Steven Spielberg's ass trying to get him to give the Cinema Department money after they rejected him for admission so many years ago? It's hilarious to watch those ass-kissers trying to make up for that slight. (Spielberg went to Cal State, Northridge.)

Film Financing Conferences - Where the money really isn't

I'm sure you've gotten, or are getting, flyers in the mail about these film financing "conferences." "Come pay your admission and we'll have real industry experts and investment people on all our panels. We're going to tell you how to do this right." Beware.

There used to be a film financing conference in San Francisco called IFFCON (the International Film Financing Conference), and it was a good one. I learned a lot. You had to have a project and apply to get in. It was tough to get in and a lot of the people there had long track records. The first year I applied, I was rejected. But on the first day, panel discussions were open to everyone, for a price.

I went and heard a lot of panelists from all over the world talk about all sorts of possible financing deals. Whenever there was a break, it was like a piranha feed around the panelists. Everyone had a story they wanted to pitch. It was bedlam, some of my fellow filmmakers I found to be quite rude. At the end of the day, there was a little meet and greet cocktail hour. Most of the panelists stayed away from it. The few that did come were surrounded.

These things can get really depressing. Everyone there is on the hustle. What you really see is the business side of things, not the art. I was at one conference where they had a "Cocktail Party for Filmmakers." The filmmakers there were trying to hustle each other. They were going after each other like we were there to buy films. And it wasn't for practice.

I finally told one pushy filmmaker to leave me alone. I was more than happy to talk politics, or art, or literature, but I was not going to discuss her film or mine because I had been doing that for two days and I needed a break. Besides, they were all filmmakers, not a distributor anywhere! I sure as hell wasn't going to invest in HER movie. I had one of my own! I was going to have a drink and relax. She called me an idiot and walked away. I had a nice quiet bourbon.

Let me tell you a couple simple facts right now.

When you approach a person who's been on a panel who you want to meet, be polite. If they're not interested, don't keep pushing. Make your project pitch short and respectful. You can see it in their eyes if they're not interested. They'll probably tell you it doesn't sound like something for them. WALK AWAY! They'll appreciate it. When it comes to meeting them again and trying to pitch something else, they'll spend more time with you because you showed them respect.

Angry Filmmaker's note: There is a thing called "an elevator pitch." You need to be able to get your film pitch down to the time it takes for an elevator to go from the first floor to the third floor. You need to make your pitch so tight that if you stumble across an executive, an actor, producer, or whomever, you can tell them enough about your movie in a few short moments to get them interested and want to talk with you.

Moreover, don't hand people demo reels and all sorts of material. They've flown in from somewhere and don't want to haul a ton of proposals and DVDs back home with them. If they're interested, ask how you can follow up. "Can I send some material to your office?"

The important aspect of these film financing conferences is to meet people and make contacts. You're not going to sell anything that day, or that week! It just doesn't happen. Keep in touch, and maybe in a few years something might work out.

The following year I was accepted into IFFCON, and that's when it got good. They accepted a limited number of projects. After the first madhouse day, I had another day-and-a-half of private meetings, smaller panels, and lots of get-together opportunities. I met some great filmmakers and made some contacts. Did I ever get my movie off the ground? NO! So I kept trying.

I started applying to the IFFM (Independent Feature Film Market) in New York. I was accepted three times. It is another large international buyers market of independent films and videos held once a year at the Angelika Theater. It used to be seven days of screenings from 9 am to 5 pm.

The first time I was accepted, it was in a new section called NO BORDERS, which was for filmmakers who had ideas and maybe demo reels but still needed funding. This section was small like IFFCON, and I spent my week doing a lot of one-on-one meetings with distributors and funding people. I was able to cement a lot of relationships with people from my earlier IFFCON days, and make more contacts. It was all part of my master plan to have my first feature there within two years. Then I'd get a distribution deal and live happily ever after.

I got in two years later with my movie *Birddog*, which I self funded. We had an okay screening time and I worked my ass off publicizing the screening. We had a good turnout for a Sunday morning.

Then the big thing happened.

While I was in New York, I went over to Miramax to see one of the executives that I had worked with on *Good Will Hunting.* We had a great meeting, and he wanted me to send *Birddog* over so he could screen it there. They would send someone to the theater to pick up the print. When I got back, I told the behind-the-scenes people that Miramax was sending someone over to pick up my movie and to release it to whoever they sent. Word traveled like wildfire that Miramax was picking up a film to view that had screened earlier. I was a modest celebrity for a few hours, anyway.

Do you want to know what happened with Miramax? I'll tell you later.

Once again, I met a lot of people and made some great contacts. We talked about all sorts of stuff, and nothing ever happened.

I went back one more time (two years later) with *The Gas Cafe* and was astounded at the changes in the market. It was three weeks after September 11th 2001. There were very few buyers there that I saw. I heard many of the Europeans didn't even show up. I don't know if it's true or not, but it was a pretty slim market.

What I do know is you couldn't find buyers or representatives from the distributors anywhere. I learned later most of them were viewing videos at the library the IFFM had set up 4 blocks away. They weren't even coming to the theater! Nor were they showing up at any of the "fun" events to mingle. Everyone wears these badges around their necks, and the color of the badges lets you know if someone's a filmmaker, a distribution person, whatever. I spotted very few distributor tags the entire week.

Five times I spent a lot of money going to these big-time conferences and five times I came away with nothing but "contacts" (which are defined as people who won't return your calls or e-mails) and hopes that would eventually be dashed.

I wasn't there, but I know some years ago the Oregon Film Commission, with a couple of other groups, put together a panel on financing independent films. They had these impressive sounding people on the panel representing lots of money, and they talked for a while about this stuff.

Someone in the audience asked one of the investment guys if he ever recommended investing in a movie to his clients. He quickly answered "No." Wait a minute! These guys are talking about how to put together business plans. What they want to see. What's the best way for filmmakers to go about making their job easier when it comes to looking over all this crap. And they're not going to recommend it to their investors? That's bullshit! Why are they even on a panel discussion? These are the people you're up against! Good luck.

Pre-Sales - No One I've Ever Met

You've probably heard the term "pre-sales." It's where you go to various distributors who handle different parts of the world. They can usually be found at film conferences and events. Their deal is you pre-sell your movie to them for an advance against the theatrical, television, or DVD distribution rights in their country, geographical area, or whatever it is they're representing. You take the money they're advancing or the contract that has the amount written on it, a bank and borrow against it, so you can go out and make your movie. You finish it, give it to the distributor, pay off the bank, and you get set to make your next movie.

I have heard about these deals. I've seen panelists at conferences talk about how these deals worked and enabled people to make their movies. But I have never ever personally known someone who has done one of these deals! Ever! Do they exist? I'm told they do, but I have never had personal contact with them. Maybe the people who make and fund these deals are all on that UFO with Elvis, Big Foot and the Loch Ness Monster, waiting for it to be safe to come back to Earth again.

Okay, you've totally exhausted the suckers - I mean wealthy people - in your town, so you decide to take your business plan to LA or New York because that's where the film business is and people there want to make movies.

Angry Filmmaker's note: Actually, everyone in the business wants to make money. Making movies just happens to be the vehicle by which they do it in New York and LA. No matter what they say, they don't really care all that much about the product just so long as it sells. A buddy of mine who grew up in the business and is a really talented guy used to say, if he had been born in Detroit, he'd probably be building Buicks. His father was in the business, he's in the business. That's just the way it is.

There's this guy who is a friend of a friend of your father's insurance agent.

Maybe you know someone whose cousin works at Fine Line, or Fox, or a small company on the Sony lot. They have a deal because their company made a movie with some guy who used to be on *Saturday Night Live.* It made a ton of money. Now they can do whatever they want.

If you can get into see these people, you'll have a great meeting. You'll walk out thinking they're really interested. Then you'll never hear from them again. If you have an idea, a script, a business plan, and a contact at any film company in LA or New York, you can get a meeting. For probably half an hour and they'll make you feel good. That's their job. They take meetings, listen to pitches, fill in spaces on their calendars, and say NO! Don't take it personally, it's just their job.

Since you're a filmmaker, you've written your script and budgeted it. Your friend is trying to raise that "easy" $3 million. You're starting to get a bit frustrated. You've been working for months and maybe even a couple of years trying to get this thing off the ground, and it's just not happening. How much money have you spent so far on not making your movie?

After I made *Birddog*, I spent months pushing another script around both LA and New York. I had all sorts of meetings with some big players, and I walked out of those rooms feeling great!

Then I couldn't get a phone call or an e-mail returned to save my life.

Remember when I sent my only film print of *Birddog* to Miramax? Well, it sat there for two months waiting to be screened. I eventually swapped it (against everyone's better judgment but my own) for a VHS tape. I needed the print for other screenings. I never have heard from Miramax about anything, and I had contacts there! It means nothing. Don't take it personally. Do you know how many people are trying to do the same thing you are?

You go back home after spending more money on these trips, and guess what? You still haven't raised a dime for your movie. Where is that "easy" $2 million dollars?

It's around this time your money-raising "friend" is probably starting to lose his or her enthusiasm. Now they're not even interested in making calls and setting up deals. "Your script seems to be the real problem," they say. Then they bail on you. But you have a contract with them, so what now? Even if you go out and raise the money yourself, you'll still have to deal with them because of that contract that says that they're the Producer, Executive Producer, or whatever. And maybe they've already put some money into the venture with the business plan and all. Now what?

If you still believe in your script and still want to make it even after all this, then work out some kind of buyout or deferment with your "former" producer and do it yourself.

CHAPTER 5:

When even Klinton Spillsbury
won't return your call: Now what?

"Face it, you are on your own."

Now that your "money raising" friend is out of the picture, your phone calls aren't being returned by anyone. And you're out a bunch of money on all of this "let's raise $3 million crap."

What's next?

Depending on the subject of your film, here's a couple of ideas.

SLASH THAT BLOATED BUDGET!

You don't need $3 million. You can make a terrific film for much less. Use the last part of that Budgeting chapter you were laughing at and realistically figure out how to make this movie.

Angry Filmmaker's note: That is if you really want to make this movie. If you just want to sit around cafes and bars and talk about it, go ahead! I don't have time for posers. This is the part of the book where we start to find out how bad you want it.

Okay, now that our expectations are much more reasonable-

If you're doing a documentary, it can be easier to raise money if you have a good idea and non-profit status.

Documentaries are so hip right now, you should find a non-profit sponsor for it. A 501(c)3 in IRS terms. I don't think you can do a dramatic feature this way, but I'm not a lawyer. Go ask one. You can also form your own non-profit corporation, but it's a lot of hassle and paperwork, and to do it right you really do need an attorney. I would only suggest forming your own nonprofit if you plan on doing a lot of documentaries or educational films. For a one-shot deal, it's too expensive and too much work.

And didn't we just learn about doing too much work and spending too much money not making your movie in the last chapter?

So what does a non-profit provide for you in return? Free money. Pure and simple. Okay, it's not really free, you're still going to have to work to get it.

You can apply to foundations, which by law can only give to non-profits. You can also solicit donations from individuals and, after discussing it with their tax professional, they can probably write the donation off on their tax return. It works wonderfully for everyone involved.

What's the downside? A non-profit will usually charge you anywhere from 5 - 8% of any funds you raise, to administer the funds and do all the bookkeeping. Some non-profits won't allow you to go after the same foundations that they're pursing, and they certainly won't help by giving you their contacts. Those are about the only downsides I've encountered.

You're going to work just as hard at raising money as you would for any other project. It's just that you aren't dealing with investors in this case, and no one expects your movie to make any money.

On one of my unfinished films, I needed to do a shoot in Bowling Green, Ohio, and I had no money. I needed to do this shoot to keep my credibility intact with my subject. So two weeks before I was to leave, I made phone calls to about 25 people I knew, and in two nights I raised just over $1200. It was enough money for me to do the shoot and keep my credibility intact.

The big selling points for me were: It was a donation from my friends that they could write off at tax time and they were helping me. The personal thing will get you further than anything else. If your friends and family won't help you, why should anyone else?

I have also thrown fundraising parties. You get a few of your friends together to host an event at their homes and have them invite friends of theirs. You all eat appetizers, drink cheap wine, and then you make a little presentation about your movie and pass the hat. These can be really successful, or not. It all depends on how aggressive you want to be.

An excellent resource for planning fundraising parties is Morrie Warshawski's book, The Fundraising House Party. Morrie is a buddy of mine, and this is a shameless plug! It's also a good book, check it out at www.morriewarshawski.com.

There are people who hate asking their friends for money. They won't do it, even in the form of a donation. These people are not going to be making movies any time soon.

We did a fundraiser once at a restaurant and all sorts of

moneyed people were there. It was organized by a professional group and the woman who was sponsoring it wanted to keep everything "low-key." Well, it was so "low-key" that we didn't make any fucking money!

It would have been better to just give me the money they spent on the fundraiser! I did follow up with thank-yous and reminders, and all sorts of stuff and made maybe $2,000, total. The event cost around $5,000. I found out later it was not so much a fundraising event as a social gathering for the people sponsoring it. Sort of a "coming out" party, if you will.

If you're going to do these kinds of fundraisers, you have to be aggressive! You have a captive audience, now you need to bag them. The next time I do it, trust me, it'll be a lot different.

There are stories that Michael Moore had Bingo parties in Michigan as one way he raised money for *Roger and Me.* I don't know how true this is. It's probably just another rumor perpetrated by the liberal media.

Which leads us back to the dramatic feature film world.

You now have a reasonable budget for your movie. What's your next step? Call your friends and family and ask them for money. It doesn't have to be a lot. You want to use their money for the next few steps. If you come from a wealthy family, then the task is a lot easier. If you come from a family that's of modest means, you're going to have to work harder.

Birddog and a deep dark hole

When I made *Birddog* in 1999, I did something really stupid. I paid almost the entire $150,000 budget myself. I had just finished the sound on *Good Will Hunting* and had all of this

94

enthusiasm and the support of a couple of well-connected people, or so I thought. I took every dime I had, got a few friends to come up with some other cash, and that was enough to shoot the movie. I cut every deal known to humankind and made a good movie in 35mm just like all of the industry professionals told me I should. It was a huge mistake! A mistake I'm still paying for.

One I put that much money together was to not pay my taxes for the year. I figured I could make the movie, get a distribution deal, pay everyone, including the tax folks and whatever penalties I owed, and it would be no big deal. It would also be a great story for the media.

WRONG!

I totally screwed up. How? I listened to people who I thought were my friends and would help me. No one ever made any concrete promises, but there was this general excitement behind the film and everyone (I thought) was really looking forward to "my breakthrough."

I do not regret making *Birddog*. I think it was something I needed to do. I had always told myself that I didn't want to be this 50-year-old guy sitting in a bar somewhere saying "You know, I coulda made a movie," into my beer as everyone moves away from me. It was a gamble. I took it and I lost!

The IRS has no sense of humor!

Seven years later I was still paying off the IRS and the Oregon Department of Revenue. On some days, I was totally stressed out and felt like there was a giant anvil above my head. I finally sold my home of 20 years to pay off everyone.

I do <u>NOT</u> recommend doing what I did!

I was in love with the notion of making an independent movie. I didn't pay attention to the part of me that kept saying, "What if this doesn't work out? What if people don't help you?" I had successful people all around me and a good track record with my short films. What could go wrong?

I always thought that I'd make my first feature with two or three other people and all of our gear in the back of a pickup truck. Instead, I got whisked away by the whole idea of shooting 35mm and having a big crew, etc. I spent way too much money!

I cut a lot of deals that were still too big for the scale that I was working on. I got a 35mm camera package donated and an incredible deal on a 5-ton Grip truck and generator. I cut deals on film stock and the film-to-tape transfers. Everything I could cut a deal on, I did. I was pretty good. And I rehearsed the cast like crazy. I wasn't taking any chances.

The Independent Film World is Full of Liars

When we showed the film, everyone liked it. The problem was, there were no big-name actors! I foolishly thought, "It's an independent movie, you don't need big names." I was wrong!

This is the way the independent film world works, so you'd better get used to it. They don't want good stories with unknowns. No one ever complained about the story, the camera work, or even the acting. In fact, no one ever guessed that it was my first feature or that the budget was only $150,000. No one! Everyone thought we spent $1.5 million.

I spent more than a year trying to get a distributor and to get financing for my next film. I screened in New York, Los

Angeles, Toronto, even London. I sent tapes to everyone I could think of and I heard the same thing over and over: "It's a good movie, but without stars, we can't sell it."

No one said the film looked lousy, the acting was bad, the story sucked. No one! What they did say was that I couldn't make a film as cheaply as I had. You just can't do that! I was told by everyone in the know that next time I needed at least one recognizable actor, and I had to spend more money.

I thought long and hard about all of this advice.

The Gas Cafe and Why "Indie" Film Can Go Fuck Itself

In 2001, Bruce Lacey and I decided to see if we could make a feature for $1,000. I had read all of the books and articles about cheap filmmaking and had funded stuff on the cheap for a long time. Now was the time to put my theory to the test. A $1,000 feature.

We failed miserably.

Our budget ballooned up to $4,000 because we had to feed people.

So how do you make a feature-length movie for $4,000? First and foremost, you DON'T use name actors! You set your entire movie in a single location, and shoot the entire thing in nine days, or nine nights, as in our case. Remember when I said I think about the budget even when I'm writing? *The Gas Cafe* was designed to be shot for NO MONEY! And that's what we did.

We started with the premise that we'd have only four characters for the entire movie, and it would take place in real time, or as close to real time as possible.

One day I was walking at the river, and a fifth character jumped out of my head fully formed. I knew there was going to be trouble. But we went ahead and made the film anyway.

What is *The Gas Cafe* about? Five people collide in a bar one night. One is dead. One never lived. And the other three are lying. (Now that's a great elevator pitch.)

Bruce and I supplied the original $1,000, ($500 each). As our food budget rose, we hit our checking accounts to get through production.

We did NOT charge anything on credit cards. That's bad! Don't do it! Sell your blood first! Since we paid for the whole thing out of our own pockets we were very careful about where we spent money. Even in the middle of production, we tried to keep a lid on expenses.

To say we failed in making a $1,000 movie sounds funny because our final budget was so much lower than the bottled-water budget for most movies.

I had read an article in American Cinematographer years earlier about a film called *Last Night at the Alamo*. It was shot by a friend of mine, Eric Edwards. The whole movie took place in a bar. Eric hung all of his lights from the ceiling. He was able to leave them up when they weren't shooting so that at night when the bar closed he was able to walk in, turn off their lights and turn his on.

We did the same thing. We took one night for nothing but a pre-light and lit the entire bar. Randy Timmerman, the DP, had one light on a stand he pulled around for close-ups. He used it as an eye light, (when we just wanted to add a little highlight to a character's face), it took a few minutes to adjust and we were shooting again.

It worked great for a lot of shooting in a short period of time. It was also good for the actors. They didn't have to wait a long time between set-ups so they were much fresher. There were times when we did have to make lighting changes, but over all, our set-up time between scenes was minimal.

We had a lot of props in the bar, pictures and signs on the wall to give it an odd feeling. We were allowed to keep those things on the walls during the time that the bar was open. So when the bar closed, we could get in there and be ready to shoot within 45 minutes (after the first night, of course, because the first night is always a cluster fuck).

We had one night of exteriors at a different location. I'd like to say that we did everything in our original nine days, but we didn't. I have to admit we had to go back three weeks later and knock off two scenes that we didn't have time to shoot. To go back in and shoot later was really bad. It was a pain to re-light what we needed, and to get the actors all pumped up again. Shoot everything as close to the schedule as you can. Once a film is wrapped, your cast, crew, and even the director loses a lot of the emotion for their project. Even in a few weeks, things are different. The camaraderie isn't there. It's a bitch.

We finished the movie, and it bombed! There you have it. I like the movie, many people don't, but it was a movie I had to make.

I sent it out to film festivals, even those that call themselves underground and experimental. They wouldn't take it. They told me it wasn't the acting or the technical aspects of the movie. It was the script. No one said it was a bad script, it was the subject matter. It made people uncomfortable.

That's what you get when you make a movie about a bunch of characters sitting around talking about death, sex and religion.

People in the U.S. get real funny when you make a movie about God, unless it's a comedy.

There is something about religion that makes people take sides and get hostile instead of trying to understand someone else's point of view. Some of my friends really like the movie because of the issues it explores and the characters. Others hate it! The amazing thing was that so many people wouldn't even discuss it.

So if you want to make an independent film questioning God and religion, and your name is not Mel Gibson, you better figure no one is going to touch it.

The interesting thing is that *The Gas Cafe* sells well on my website and when I tour. A lot of film students send me notes telling me how much they like it. And they understand the humor, which is very dark, but that was the point. So, maybe we did okay after all.

Kicking Bird and the Feeling of Liberation

For *Kicking Bird,* I tried something different as far as funding. I sent letters to everyone I knew, friend or not, and asked them for $100 each. I figured I could get 100 people to send me $100. I could make a movie on $10,000. The downside was I didn't really know 100 people. I topped out at 77. I still sent the letters out and raised $5200 in just a few weeks.

Here is a copy of the letter.

December 15, 2003

Dear Gus,

Well, it's Angry Filmmaker time again. In fact, it's past time.

I haven't made a film in two years and I have a script that's just dying to be produced. So it's time to hit all my friends up for money and find out how few friends I really have.

When the Republicans and the Democrats are trying to raise money they always come up with some catchy name for the bribes, I mean donations, that they're receiving like The Gemstone 500, or The Kitchen Cabinet. But I know that you're too smart and cynical for a cheap ploy like that. What I'm trying to do is find 100 people who are willing to give me $100 each. One hundred people, $100. That means a total of $10,000 to shoot my new feature. And we've even come up with a catchy name for our group of supporters. "One Hundred People Who Should Really Know Better." Because by now, you really should.

So if you send me money, and I get to make my film you're probably asking yourself, "What do I get out of this?" Well, I'm glad you asked. In addition to my undying friendship and thanks, (and probably another letter just like this one next year), you get your name in the credits and two tickets to the premiere of the movie. And if we raise enough money, we might even have a party after the screening (i.e., a cheap Brie wheel and a six pack of Hamms). So what are you waiting for?

Seriously, I feel I have a really good script and I know I can assemble the talent to pull this movie off for $10,000. I am also fortunate to have some good friends that so far have committed $2000. So if you want to give more than $100, please. I appreciate it. And if you can't give me any money then maybe you can help me in other ways. I have a list of locations, equipment, props and services we're going to need. Maybe you can help me with some of those things.

Oh, and Harris (you know, my attorney) wants me to tell you

that the $100 is not tax deductible. It is considered a gift.
And no, you don't own a piece of the movie. Just nice seats at
the premiere.

If you have any questions, or just want to pull my chain a bit,
call me. For accounting purposes please make checks out to
Square One Productions, Inc., and designate that it's for the
film, *KICKING BIRD*.

Thank you very much.

Sincerely,
Kelley

Here's the trick with the letter. It was funny, all the people knew
me, and I wasn't asking for much. All I was promising were
their name in the credits and two seats at the premiere. (The
credit reads, "49 People Who Should Really Know Better.")
They weren't getting ownership of the movie in any way, shape
or form. Just two tickets.

The amazing part was how many people who could easily afford
to give me $100, didn't. And how quickly they forgot they
hadn't when I ran into them later. Sometimes they'd ask if
I could re-send the letter, sometimes they just ignored the whole
subject. But I raised $5,200 and shot the movie. I included a
stamped self-addressed envelope so that it was really easy for
them to send me a check back.

There was one person who never responded and then sent me
some information that I had to fill out for her organization. She
sent me the forms using my very own self-addressed stamped
envelope. She thought it was funny. I thought it was tacky. If
she would have cut the stamp off of the envelope and used it on
a letter to someone else, I would never have known. By sending

me forms from her organization, using my stamp and envelope, I felt like she didn't take me seriously.

You need to make it as easy as possible for people to help you out. Never get mad about something, just figure out another angle. How much food can you get donated? Getting the coffee donated doesn't seem like much, but on a three week-shoot we saved a few hundred dollars. On a $5,000 budget, that's huge.

Sometimes It's Not About the Money

Some of my friends really couldn't afford the $100. I know, I know, I hang out with some real deadbeats, but they wanted to help in some way. Many of them came through with other things that helped the production run smoother. All of our still film was donated, as well as the processing and printing. We were given free pastries and breakfast stuff from a small bakery. My hairstylist even promised to give me $100 worth of free haircuts if that would help. We got good deals on everything.

All you have to do is ask. Remember, "Don't ask, don't get." LIVE BY THAT PHRASE.

When you're asking for things, remember to tell people the magic words, "I'm making a film." A lot of people are donating lots of time and working hard to make the script a reality. When they are working this hard on a creative endeavor, there is a certain dignity to it. I'm not sure why, but people respond. I am always amazed at the outpouring of help for my movies.

Remember, you have to get creative. Whatever you do, don't cut back on food for the crew.

What else can you hustle for free? You probably have friends who know someone who can get you something you need.

If you need a particular prop, location, car, almost anything, ask around. When we needed a bunch of old car props on *Birddog*, my production designer found a little cafe that had a bunch of old parts as part of their design. We were able to use a ton of stuff for free.

When you start hustling, it's amazing what you can come up with. Like I said earlier, people really do want to help you. They just need to be asked.

Figure out everything you're going to need. Make a Wish List, then start asking. Make sure everyone knows if they can't help you right now, it's no big deal. Don't hold grudges or say bad things about them. Go make your movie, and next time around, ask them again. If they see you out there doing it, with or without their help, they just might want to be involved next time.

And if your "it's easier to raise two million dollars than a million" buddy calls, don't answer it. It'll only piss you off.

So, what's next?

CHAPTER 6:

LET'S GET ORGANIZED...

"Now that you've decided to go ahead and shoot this damn thing, remember you don't care what the so-called "independent community" thinks. Screw them! They're the first ones to call you stupid, and the first to show up for any success you might have."

Let's break this thing down and figure out when and how we're going to shoot this monster.

How long do you think it's going to take to shoot this thing? All my features have been shot in less than three weeks. I figure, if you're going to have people help you on your movie, any more than three weeks is pushing it for free help.

Angry Filmmaker's note: Many classic films were shot in fewer than 18 days. Some old studio films were shot in 10 to 15 days. It has only been recently, with bloated budgets and everyone wanting to be like Francis Coppola, that shoots have gone way over schedule. It's amazing how much you can get accomplished with a small crew on a short schedule if you organize everything and rehearse your actors like crazy.

Let's start with the script and figure out how we're going to make the best use of everyone's time. There are programs available that will help break it down for you. So, before you start plugging stuff in, you need to know what the hell you're doing.

Paint by numbers

The first thing you need to do is number your scenes. This can be done in a variety of ways, but remember, once you do it and print out your script, these numbers are permanent. These numbers will be with you from pre-production all the way through post-production. You can't change them. You need to do it right the first time, after that you can modify them, but never, ever change them.

The way I start my numbering is by days. Not shoot days, but the days in the script. I start with the number 101. Scene 101 means the first day of the story in the script, the first scene. Scene 102 means the first day, second scene. Then I use letters: 101 is usually a Master shot, 101A is the next angle, 101b the next, and so on, until I have the entire scene covered.

Always start with your wide shots, then move in for close-ups and cutaways. Standardize your working method so you don't have to think about it. You just do it.

This accomplishes several things. Anyone can look at the scene number and know what day it is in the story. Since we're shooting out of sequence, the scene numbers help keep continuity straight, like wardrobe, makeup (in the case of before or after a fight scene, does an actor have a black eye, or has it partially healed?) and what props are needed for the scene. The numbering also tells you how many scenes are in a certain "script" day.

This is the numbering system that I use on the slate when I'm shooting. The sound people will use this information on their logs, and the editor will live and die by this information when editing the movie.

If done right, it will save both the picture editor and the sound editors lots of time. Never scrimp here. Take your time and do the numbering right.

This is not the only way to number a script, it's the way I do it. This method might not work for you. Figure out a variation that you can use, then stick to it.

The Breakdown (Not Yours, the Movie's)

For those who want to do it on their own, without a computer, this is the old-style. Print out all of your script tag lines (these are your locations at the beginning of each scene, for example, Interior - Dad's Restaurant - Day) and cut them into strips. Put them in piles according to location first. If you're shooting a bunch of scenes at Dad's Restaurant, put those together. The scenes at the school should go together, and so on. Then separate each pile in to night and day strips. Start laying the strips out in order by location, day, or night.

This is like an art project because you're going to lay out the strips and tape them to sheets of paper in an organized manner. You can buy a "professional breakdown" board that comes with cardboard strips to write on, then you lay it out on the board that has plastic liners. It's much easier than scotch tape, but not as artistic.

If you're shooting days and nights in the same location, ask yourself how much time you need to shoot these scenes. Avoid the 14-hour day. I try to keep my days to 10 hours, 11 at the most. Your people are working for FREE!!! Be nice to them.

Angry Filmmaker's note: You're not going to get much accomplished the first day of shooting. That's when a lot of logistic problems and all sorts of other stuff starts happening. Make sure you plan at least two light days later in your shooting schedule so you can shoot a few scenes you've missed to get back on schedule.

I like shooting in the winter because of the short daylight hours. Since the sun goes down early (if it shows up at all in Oregon), I can split a shoot day between a day and night scene. If you try to do that in the summer, your day begins around 3 in the afternoon. It doesn't get dark until around 10 p.m. In the winter, I can start at 10 or 11 a.m. and shoot a day scene. It gets dark around 4:30 pm, then I can start shooting night scenes.

With *The Gas Cafe,* the whole movie takes place in a single location at night. We blacked out the windows (hung black plastic over the windows) so that we could shoot at anytime and it was always night in the bar. In reality it was two locations, one interior and one exterior.

We still had to break down the script to figure out what scenes should be shot when. Since we purposely planned it for one location, all at night, it made things simpler as far as scheduling things, setup times and a consistent cast and crew call.

We always knew when we could start and finish because we could only shoot when the bar was closed.

Angry Filmmaker's note: The only schedule problem we ever had on *The Gas Cafe* was a train schedule. There are train tracks right next to the real bar, and every night around 4 a.m. a train came down the tracks moving box cars around. It would sit idling next to the bar for about 30 minutes. I think they sat out there longer just to piss me off. There was no way we could shoot because the entire building shook. I knew about the train ahead of time, but was told they weren't in the area very long. Liars!

I knew the last night was going to be the longest. We had

more scenes to shoot than any other night, so I put all the exteriors at the end of our shooting schedule. By the last night of shooting, the crew was a well-oiled machine and everything went pretty smoothly. We started around 9 p.m. and finished just before sunrise.

Angry Filmmaker's note: Never put the final scene, big climactic scenes, or any love scenes early in your shooting schedule if you can avoid it. These scenes are always tough to shoot from an acting standpoint. There's nothing worse than throwing two actors into a love scene early on, and saying, "Okay, take your clothes off in front of strangers and start making love!" It's not going to be a very good scene. Also, if a couple of characters are going to have a major fight with each other, give them time to get into rhythm and character on the set before you demand that they emote their brains out.

Your crew is still getting to know how each other works, and you haven't set up a good working pace yet. Get the cast and crew comfortable with each other before the really tough scenes.

Don't be afraid to have a "closed" set when doing intense scenes. By "closed," I mean only the people who are absolutely necessary. Get the rest of the cast and crew members away from where you're shooting. You don't want extra distractions for your actors while they're working on a scene that might be uncomfortable for them, which usually happens with love scenes or anything with nudity. Your actors will thank you for closing the set, but half the crew will be pissed. That's okay. Any cast or crew person who gets pissed about a closed set because of nudity shouldn't be there in the first place.

On big movies, other people always do the script breakdown. Assistant directors, some producers, or sometimes production coordinators. Well, you can't afford that. So get used to doing it yourself. I always work with my DP (Randy Timmerman) because from a photographic standpoint, he knows how long it's going to take to light and shoot various scenes, how fast his crew can move, and what scenes can be lumped together for efficiency. Randy has a great feel for this sort of thing. I keep in mind the order of the scenes and how tough they will be on the cast because I want to get the most out of the actors. Start small and work up as everyone gets more comfortable working together.

When changing your schedule from days to nights, or nights to days, give the cast and crew at least 8 hours of turnaround time (time when they can sleep, or just be off the set), I think 10 hours works best.

You can't be shooting nights and say, "Okay it's 2 a.m. Let's start shooting days. See you all at 8 a.m." The soonest you should start would be 10 a.m. If you can make your transition from shooting nights to shooting days over your days off, that works best. Once again, treat your crew right, and they'll work hard for you.

When you're thinking about your shoot schedule, remember, your cast or crew probably have regular jobs. Some might be worried about turning down paying work while they're working on your movie for free.

I plan my shoots to go from Wednesday through Sunday. Most commercial film jobs don't happen on weekends because clients and agency people really hate working on the weekends. If two of your main shooting days each week occur on the weekend, then your cast and crew has to worry only about three days they're unavailable for other work.

Since they're working for free, if they get a day job or a few days' worth of work, I always tell them to do it. You can't have people give up paying work to help you. We all have to eat!

I have found that most of the time when someone has to leave for a few days they find their own replacement to cover. That shows they care about your movie and they are true professionals. They are the kind of crew people I like, and when I have paying work, these are the first people I hire. They've proved themselves to me.

Permit Hell

I am not a fan of bureaucracy. I hate permits and dealing with the city, state, or whoever requires permits or permission for shooting in public places. If I have scenes that are on public property, I check my calendar and make sure I can shoot the scene with the least amount of bullshit possible.

On *Kicking Bird,* the local school district wanted too much money (as far as I'm concerned) to shoot at one of their EMPTY schools! We kept looking around until we found a school outside the city that was happy to let us shoot there. FOR FREE!

The school was too rural for our exterior shots, although they were glad to accommodate us. Not only were they excited about having us shoot at their school, but they also handed out flyers to all of the drama students outlining when we would be shooting. On both days of our schedule at the school, we had about 50 kids who stayed after school to be extras. It worked out great!

For the exteriors, the school that had everything I wanted was in the city and in the perfect neighborhood. Since this was a movie about running, it also had a track (and this was the best part) located 2 blocks away from the school. That meant I could shoot track scenes on a Saturday or Sunday and no teachers or administrators would be wandering around.

The school had a great courtyard off the main street. It was secluded and had very little traffic noise. Since I would be right at the school, and sometimes they have weekend programs or teachers and administrators working on the weekends, what could I do?

January has a three-day weekend. Martin Luther King Jr.'s birthday. I planned my shoot at the school for the Sunday of the three-day weekend. My figuring was, if the faculty or staff had any work to catch up on, they would go to the school on either Saturday or Monday, so that they could still have a two-day weekend.

We shot for 7 hours. We had 35-40 extras. We had the whole place to ourselves. None of the neighbors asked us any questions. We even staged a fight. We got in, we shot, we got the performances we needed, and we cleaned up after ourselves. I'm sure no one at that school had any idea there had been a film crew there.

For the final race, I wanted to use a really nice track in a different part of town. Ordinarily, you would need a permit. Instead of asking, we scheduled that shoot for a Sunday, Super Bowl Sunday, to be precise. I knew there were not going to be city employees there that day. We did have a crew show up. They cleaned the bathrooms for us. They were really nice, wished us luck, and took off.

Since we looked like we knew what we were doing , so no one asked us anything. We were polite and stayed out of the other runners' ways until it was time for us to shoot our big event. By that time most of the other runners had left, probably to go get beer and chips for the game. We had the place to ourselves. I promised the cast and crew we would be done by 4 that day so that those who wanted could go watch most of the game. And we were.

I hate permits and dealing with bureaucracy, but I am extremely careful about when and where I shoot. I stay out of people's way, and we ALWAYS clean up the area better than we found it!

Angry Filmmaker's note: One of the biggest mistakes new filmmakers make is not allowing enough time for pre-production. There seems to be this myth that if you're not actually shooting, then you are not making your movie. I have found over and over, the more time I spend in pre-production, which includes casting, scheduling, and location scouting, the smoother and more efficiently my shoots run. Figure out how long you need for pre-production, then double or triple it! Remember, it's a big deal making a movie. Treat it like one.

Murphy Works Harder Than You Do

Lay out your schedule on the board, sheets of paper, or whatever. That way you have a place to start. Show it to other "experienced" crew people and get their feedback. Make changes accordingly. Remember, the shooting schedule is a living, breathing thing. It's going to change while you're working. You're not going to have enough time to finish a location, something is going to fall through, actors will get sick or have conflicts, you'll lose locations, or whatever. It's going to happen and you have to be ready to shift things around and shoot in a different order than what you might have planned.

Try to have back-up locations you can go to if something changes at the last minute. If you get rain on an exterior and you don't want it, have an interior you can go shoot instead. I love the rain. The crappier and darker the day, the happier I am. It fits my style. In the Northwest, the weather can change dramatically in just a few minutes. You need to be ready for it. I usually get screwed by the weather being nice. I really hate that!

Look at your schedule and think about how much you can accomplish with a minimum of hassle. It will save you money, and that's what this is all about.

Remember, there is a lot more to scheduling than just plugging scenes into days.

The Fine Art of Casting

Let's cast this monster. I always cast on weekends; more actors are available and it's easier to schedule time. I always have certain actors in mind when I write, but there are always lots of other roles to fill.

On **Birddog** and **The Gas Cafe**, I used video for the auditions, on **Kicking Bird** I didn't. Using tape was all well and good, but by the third movie, I was confident enough that I knew what I was looking for. I have final say anyway, so I didn't feel the need for video. I have a great casting director (Louanne Moldovan) who always brings me great people. So casting goes pretty quickly for me.

In **The Gas Cafe** we have nudity. That made casting a bit different for two of the roles. I told every prospective actor about the nudity ahead of time and that it was NOT gratuitous. It was a plot point I felt was important. I explained the plot point and the motivation to them. If they had a problem with it, then they could leave, no problems. Most actors stayed.

I have heard stories where actors tell you nudity is no problem, until you hire them and start shooting. Some actors wait until you get to that scene, then they refuse to do it. As a filmmaker, you're stuck. You've already committed a lot of time and resources to your movie, and now you have an actor who won't do the scene the way you've always imagined it.

114

You can either pull the plug on the actor, re-cast and re-shoot everything they've appeared in, (yeah right), or you can try to convince them your vision is good. If you're doing that this far into the production, you're really screwed. Or, you can figure out an alternative to the scene and be pissed off at that actor for the rest of the shoot and through all of eternity. As much as I like anger, that's not a good use of it.

When I did call-backs, I decided to have two actors (male and female) together for a regular scene and the nude scene. They were going to have to be able to take their clothes off in the casting sessions. I also wanted to see how comfortable they were together in that particular situation.

I prepared the actors to do the scene in the call-backs. I also pulled the camera out of the auditions so there was no tape. I made sure that there were both males and females in the room (usually one of the producers), and kept the casting session very small and private. I don't want anyone coming back and telling me I handled anything unprofessionally. I want witnesses! It's just a precaution, and everyone I've worked with has been very cool about it. I've never had any problems with nudity or actors freaking out on me. It's all about respecting the actors.

Once you cast your actors, have them write down their work schedules. Ask them about their flexibility. You need to take this into consideration for scheduling. There's nothing worse than an actor not showing up for a scene.
In *Birddog,* we found out that one of the actors went to LA for an audition and wouldn't be back in time for his scene. He told us that was the way it was, and we would have to reschedule the scene around his schedule. From what I heard, he was arrogant when the producer talked to him.

I recast him. Who needs that shit! He wasn't the lead and,

actually, he wasn't my first choice for that role. The first actor had had a scheduling conflict. I had the AD call the first actor back to see if he still had a scheduling conflict. He was thrilled that we called him back and was able to change his schedule. I got the actor I wanted, stayed on schedule, and basically told the arrogant actor to piss off.

We now have a cast, everyone's schedules, and we know what we want to shoot when.

Rehearse Until You Drop

Do as much rehearsing as humanly possible. The more you rehearse the better the actors know their parts. Note that I said parts, not lines. The actors have to be comfortable with their characters. They have to have the opportunity to question you about everything that has to do with their character. I write character bios as part of my script-writing process. I share these bios with the actors so they have a better idea where these people come from and what they may or may not be thinking about.

I want the actors to flesh out these characters, and the more I do in rehearsal, the less I have to do on the set. By the time we get to the set, I want everyone to be their character. When we get to the set, we can quickly block the scene, send the cast to makeup and wardrobe, and the crew can start setting lights.

Road Trip

My DP and I always go to the locations ahead of time, together.

We always look at where the power is (electrical) and what lights and props we can steal from the location. I don't really mean steal, I mean what we can use that we won't have to bring in. I like to bring the production designer and the gaffer when

116

possible. They always have good ideas on what we can and can't get away with as far as power, existing light, and props.

In *Birddog*, we were checking out the bank branch for one of the scenes, and it was my production designer who suggested an angle to shoot. We wouldn't have to move any furniture, and I could get the huge vault in the background. This saved us a lot of time on a very tight shoot day.

I don't use storyboards because I can't draw worth shit. I never have the budget to hire someone. What I do with Randy is a lighting diagram. We figure out what the action of the scene is going to be, where we want the actors, and then we discuss where the lights should go. We do this when we're checking out the location prior to the shoot day.

I don't want to waste everyone's time on the day of the shoot, looking at a location and trying to figure out what I want. However, there are times you get to the location and have to change what you originally planned. It can be for a lot of reasons, but if you have a diagram from your first visit, you have something to work from. No shoot ever goes perfectly, but you should try to be as prepared as possible.

I also do shot lists. I write down all of the different angles I want to get. Wide shots, mediums, two shots, close-ups, whatever. Then I can cross-reference my lists with my diagrams.

And most important: I use a SCRIPT SUPERVISOR!

I always like to meet ahead of time with the script supervisor. I give them notes, lists, whatever I have. They will keep you on the right track. They're the ones who will line the script for you as you're shooting. They'll make sure that you get coverage on

117

every scene. They'll take notes as to camera rolls, sound rolls, and what takes you liked. The good ones also ride herd on the breakdown and make, sure since you're shooting out of sequence, that you get everything you need and that the editor gets everything they need. We like script supervisors. If they're good, they can save your ass.

I have to go back to the permit/permission thing one more time. It all depends on where you're shooting and what you're doing. I was shooting a corporate video for Freightliner Trucks (a division of Mercedes Benz), and we had a scene to shoot in Canada. I told the producer and the people involved with the production that if we were going to shoot in Canada, we would need work permits for the crew. I had worked in Canada before. We would also need customs brokers to get our gear (including a brand new semi truck and trailer) in and out of Canada.

The script called for a shot of the truck rolling off the ferry in Victoria and the driver having a conversation with a Canadian Mountie at Customs. Well, the people at Freightliner fucked up! We got off the ferry and there were customs brokers waiting for us, but no one had gotten us work permits! After a long conversation with a guy from Immigration, we were denied entrance to Canada. We were turned back! We had to wait for the next ferry and go back to the U.S. without shooting.

Not only was I pissed about the lack of planning, but my DP and I now have a record with Immigration. This has turned into a hassle for me on trips out of the country. Whenever I go out of the country or return from abroad, I'm stopped because my name pops up in the immigration computers. I get questioned, I have to explain the whole thing and eventually they let me through because my paperwork is current and correct! I demanded that the people at Freightliner fix this error through their attorneys. It never was and the people I used to work with over there were all laid off during one of their many corporate restructurings.

The people who worked for Freightliner on the shoot were not penalized, only the freelancers because Freightliner has offices in Canada. Basically, the Immigration guy was a prick. But the real blame lies with the people from Freightliner for not doing their homework after I informed them what was needed!

I take some blame because I didn't check everything out before we left. But I was also shooting another piece for them and was home for less than a day before we took off for Canada. Even though I was assured that everything was fine, I should have checked again. Trust no one!

When I was in Paris years ago I wanted to shoot scenics of the city for a film I was working on. We were told that if we shot any of Paris's landmarks, we would have to have a permit. I remember someone telling us if we shot with a tripod we needed to have a permit, and the cops would stop us and fine us if we got caught.

I talked to the desk clerk at our hotel, who suggested I hire his cousin, a cab driver. I wanted to shoot the city at night. I figured that would look much more romantic for the movie. The cab driver took my DP and me to all the places I wanted, and he even showed us some angles of landmarks I hadn't seen before. He kept the cab idling and watched for the police. It turned out to be a great shoot, and it cost me about $400. It was well worth it. We also shot some scenics during the day. We used an old Canon Scoopic. (Good luck finding one of those anymore.) The Canon is a 16mm camera that shoots 100-foot spools. It looks like an amateur home movie camera. The Canon was so light that we shot everything hand-held. We didn't even take a tripod with us. We wanted to blend in as much as possible.

We were only bothered once, by a street vendor. We quietly apologized and walked away.

The Paris shoot happened before the Freightliner debacle. Would I try to shoot in a foreign city again without permits since I have a record? I don't know. Ask me again when I am thrust into that situation. I do know that when I travel abroad for any reason I am much more careful about everything I do. The idea of being thrown into a foreign jail or detention center and then being expelled does not interest me at all. Having a record with the Immigration authorities is not pleasant. And it is permanent.

So, if you ever have to shoot anything outside the US, find out about the laws and what will be required of you when you get there.

Oh my God! We have our script broken down, our locations nailed, actors cast, and the crew hired. Now what? It's time to scam some gear.

CHAPTER 7:

EQUIPMENT: Out of the Box & Obsolete

"Whatever you buy is going to be obsolete by the time you get it out of the box!"

It's not going to be worth shit! Why did you just spend your hard-earned money on this stuff?

DO NOT go to the video store to buy equipment! The salespeople always want you to buy the latest and the greatest. It helps their bottom line, not yours! Remember, these people have no lives, and that's why they're techno-sales geeks! Many of them don't own any gear themselves, they just know what other people should own.

Have you ever heard of the term "commission?" That's what these people get. The more gear they sell you, the bigger their commission. If you think about it, the equipment really hasn't changed all that much over the years. Film cameras still shoot at 24 frames per second and video cameras... well, video cameras are different because those idiots keep changing formats on us.

The second most frequently asked question I get is, what kind of camera do you use? God that's a stupid question! What difference does a camera make? A camera doesn't make your movie. You do!

As far as I am concerned, a camera is a tool. It's just like a hammer if you do construction. The difference in film and video is the same as water colors and oil to a painter. Different movies require different tools. I want something that will put the image I want up on the screen. I don't care the make, model or age of the gear, as long as it does what I need it to do.

A friend of mine has an old Betacam camera. It was the top-of-the-line "industrial" camera when he first got it. It ran him around $10,000 - $15,000. In my mind, that camera has a better look than a lot of digital cameras. It has a softer look than most video cameras, and when we light scenes with it, people ask me what kind of a camera we're using. They are shocked when they find out it's an old Betacam. It's not the camera, it's the lighting and everything else that goes into making a movie.

You need to learn how to spend your money wisely if you're going to make a movie. Let me tell you my method.

The Fine Art of Scamming

You can scam (or if you prefer, borrow) just about anything. Remember in an earlier chapter when I told you to be nice to people? That goes double in the equipment department. If you're a nice person and have banked lots of favors over the years, then it's time to cash them in.

If you want to shoot film, you can still get deals, but not as good as you're going to get if you shoot video.

On *Birddog*, I was extremely lucky. A fellow who has always been supportive of me and my work owns a camera rental house. He gave me, rent free, a 35 mm camera package, complete with lenses, mags, batteries, tripod, and all of the support stuff! It was great! It was not the newest gear, but it was professionally maintained, and we never had a problem. And the cost was zippo! Nada! Nothing!

Good luck trying to pull something like this off. I was lucky; my friend respected my previous work, and when I rented equipment, I was always up front with him. If I could pay full rental on a commercial job, I did. If I didn't have a big enough budget, I told him at the beginning and we worked it out. No bullshit! We have a good business relationship, even today, when I shoot more tape than film. It doesn't matter. We're friends and we do business. I respect him and it goes both ways.

Angry Filmmaker's note: There used to be these commercial producers I knew who were real sleazebags. They would rent equipment, book time, and hire people. At the end of the job, they would come back and say they didn't have enough money to pay for everything. That's when they would ask for deals! By then it was too late. Everyone was screwed! These guys would also ask for a big break in your rate and use that old come on, "Give us a break on a first job together and we'll get you your full rate on the next one." Well, there was never a next one! The film business is full of sleazebags. They are no different from a lot of people in the business that will try and take advantage of you. Beware! I always tell people, I only give breaks to my long time clients. Do three or four jobs with me and then we'll talk about a break. Assholes!

If you want to shoot 16 mm, then start looking around for an old CP 16 (Cinema Products). These cameras were the backbone of the local news stations for years and are really sturdy. They were designed and built to take abuse. There are still some of them around if you know where to look. Call someone at a TV station. A couple of cameras might still be sitting in the basement. These idiots had no idea what to do with them because as video was being phased in many were just put into storage. A lot of enterprising film programs snapped them up and still use them, so they might be tough to find.

If you can locate any of these cameras at a TV station, they'll probably part with one and its support gear for a song. They have no use for these cameras anymore. They probably don't have anyone around who knows how to thread them!

I shot all of my short films and quite a few documentaries with a wonderful old CP. They aren't Arri's or Aatons. They are a workhorse! If you want to shoot film on the cheap, this is your ticket. So what are you waiting for? The only downside to the CP 16 is that it won't shoot super 16. You need to shoot with either an Arri or an Aaton. Those cameras are out there, just not so available, and they're expensive. You're going to have to be nice to someone.

Angry Filmmaker's note: Film cameras don't become obsolete. They were built to certain specifications, 24 fps, 36 fpm (90 fpm in 35mm), and they are always going to run at that speed if you have good batteries. There are places that still fix and maintain these cameras. They are very easy to find.

Let's Go Video!

Okay, so you're going to shoot video. The last thing you ever want to do is buy a video camera! That's really pissing away money. Most of the other equipment we're going to talk about in this chapter, you can justify purchasing. Editing equipment, sound equipment, and lighting gear. All of this stuff can be used for years with a few simple upgrades. But cameras?

The manufacturers must really think we're stupid. They're always updating, coming out with new stuff, or just changing formats. How many damn video formats are there these days? How many people remember D1? That was going to be the format that changed everything. I still have a bunch of masters on D2. Hardly anyone I know still has a working D2 machine. And who can forget "M" format? Remember that? All these NBC idiots and their affiliates went out and bought that crap. Somebody is still laughing about the commissions they made on that stuff.

There are a lot of DV cameras that you can either get cheap or borrow. When the Canon XL1 came out, people were buying that one like crazy. It was the first DV camera that was affordable and had a good picture. When I shot *The Gas Cafe,* we had three of them on the set and we didn't pay for a single one. This was the most common "professional" DV camera around at the time. Everyone who wanted to be a DP or a filmmaker bought one. And because those people bought cameras, I didn't have to.

Angry Filmmaker's note: Hey Canon, would you people please fix the fucking lenses on your cameras? When you're trying to focus a Canon, the focus ring never stops! It just keeps turning! That is so frustrating on a set! Just have the fucking thing go from Point A to Point B and stop! There's nothing worse than trying to set focus on a Canon!

On *Kicking Bird*, my DP and I discussed using the new Panasonic DVX100 24p camera. We watched a camera test which looked fantastic. The grain patterns, the clarity, and although it really doesn't look like film (I don't care what anyone says, it doesn't really look like film!), it had a terrific look. Randy was all gung-ho to use it, but I said "No!" I agreed it looked great. My problem was it looked too good.

Kicking Bird is a movie about a group of kids from the poor side of town and even if they might have a future, their present is shitty. I shoot in January for the lousy weather and the dinginess of Portland. I want their surroundings to look depressing. I want these people's lives to look and feel horrible. I want the weather and their physical surroundings to be working against them. I want things to look bleak. I certainly don't want vibrant colors. I told Randy that if we were shooting film I would shoot in black and white. If we shoot with the Panasonic then when I am editing it I will drain a lot of the color out and grain it up so the look of the movie will feel like their surroundings. Why go to all of that trouble when we could use an older camera (for free) and get exactly the look I wanted while we were shooting?

We borrowed a Sony PD 150. Actually, we ended up giving the guy $300 for three weeks use. (He was a jerk! He demanded the money while we were shooting.) But it certainly was better than buying a camera. Yes, the camera was obsolete when we used it, but if I didn't tell you what kind of a camera we used, you wouldn't have guessed. I wanted something that looked gritty, and that's exactly what I got. I like the look of *Kicking Bird.*

The Lost Art of the Camera Test

The truth of the matter is, you can save a lot of money on equipment if you know what you want and are willing to use last year's model. Whenever you scam, er, borrow a camera, shoot a roll of tape with it first.

With film cameras, we always shoot tests. You want to see how tight the lens is and how sharp the picture is.

With a video camera you want to test for those things as well as what the picture looks like under different lighting situations.

126

Is it really low light? How are the sound heads? Run a test like you would on anything. If you like the way the picture looks on a borrowed camera, then screw that salesperson! Tell them they're going to have to find some other schmuck to make their quota this month, cause you're not going to do it.

Angry Filmmaker's note: Beware of any idiot that tells you that you NEED the latest stuff. This person may be in the business, but odds are, they aren't. These are "Kling-ons," as my daughter likes to call them. They're not really in the business, just hanging around the fringes. They're usually skinny with glasses and thinning hair and don't own any equipment themselves. Tell them to shut the fuck up!

They can give me advice after they've put out their own money for a bunch of gear they can't afford and have to settle for less than the top of the line! Let them buy stuff that is going to get used every day, knowing full well that by the time they get the shit unpacked, there's going to be a new toy on the market they can't afford, now that they've blown all their money.

I think, as we embark on making a movie, we are vulnerable. We want to make the best movie possible, and when someone starts telling us how we have to have something, we fall for it. You don't want to feel you're doing your movie a disservice after all the work that's gone into it so far. I mean, this is your big break! So maybe you'll consider spending the extra couple of thousand bucks.

DON'T DO IT! If it's a salesperson telling you that you NEED something, walk away! They are exploiting you.

Anyway, back to cameras. Always look around for camera people who own their own stuff. It'll save you money. Camera people, by and large, can be freaks. I had a camera instructor at

USC who was more protective of his damn light meters than he was of his wife and kids. No kidding. He'd probably let you sleep with his wife before he'd ever let you borrow his meter!

A Bright Idea

You need good lights. Good lighting is the difference between amateurs and professionals. People think because it's video, they don't need lights. Then they wonder why their stuff looks like shit! Use lights.

Lights are easy to dig up, depending on what you need. If you're looking at an entire grip truck with a generator, that's a little tougher. These things can be had, you just need to know who to approach.

A lot of people have their own lights. Some gaffers buy theirs because they can pick them up used. It saves them money, and they figure if they have some lights they'll get more work. And that's true.

Check out film schools. A lot of small film programs will have a few Arri light kits, or Lowell light kits. They are nice compact kits, and it's amazing how much you can light with them if you know what you're doing. Also look into small production companies. If they're not using their lights at the moment, they might give you a hell of a deal.

There is always borrowing from cable access. Now, I know if you use their gear, you're supposed to let them broadcast something in return. So shoot a trailer or a short video just to give them something. We'll keep the fact that you just shot a feature with their gear between the two of us.

You will also need C-stands, flags, clamps, and all sorts of other grip equipment. Keep your eyes open. It's all out there, and pretty cheap if you have to buy it. You will use this stuff over and over again, and it doesn't become obsolete. So, go get it already!

And don't forget the stingers and the C-47's. You can never have too many of either.

Angry Filmmaker's note: If you don't know what stingers or C-47's are prepare to be taken advantage of. If you are working with a lighting and grip company, they are going to charge you a fortune for C-47's. They put bags of C-47's on the grip truck. If you open one it can cost you around $20. It is always better to go out and get your own. A C-47 is a wooden clothes pin and they can be bought by the bag for under $2. Stingers are extension cords. Really big extension cords that can handle a lot of power and don't get hot. In almost every business it seems like people re-name mundane things so it sounds more impressive and they can charge you more. I am not going to pay $20 for a bag of wooden clothes pins, but I might for C-47's.

I once worked on a show where the narrator spoke about delivering your material in a specially designed "wood fiber corrugated container". It was a card board box!

Aural Fixation

Sound people always have their own equipment, so don't ever buy this stuff. Sound people, like camera people, are protective when it comes to their gear. They usually don't loan it out, or even rent it unless they go with it. In any town, there are always a few people who do sound, and they have their own stuff.

Sometimes you find someone who is trying to break into the business. They'll go out and buy equipment so people will hire them. Find these people. They're going to give you a break, and they need something for their resume. Just keep your eyes on them because of their lack of experience. We'll touch on that later.

If you have to purchase something, it is hard to go wrong with audio gear. There are still some good DAT machines out there that are reasonably priced. You can also get a Hard Disc Recorder. Many location recording mixers use these, but a lot of people I know run backup DATs as well. I'm not sure they totally trust Disc Recorders. After a good recorder, if you have to buy something, buy a really nice microphone. There are a lot of different ones out there, but microphone technology doesn't change all that much.

Angry Filmmaker's note: Let's talk sound quality for a moment. (We'll talk a lot more in the sound chapter.) This is a bad place to try to cut corners. Remember, if people can't understand the dialog in your movie, they won't watch it! I would rather see shitty camera work than listen to indecipherable dialog, and so would most people. Get a good microphone.

I have an old Sennheiser ME-80 that I bought in the late '80's that is still going strong. It's a modular system. I can use it as a shotgun microphone or I can use the lavaliere attachment. I have taken excellent care of this mic and it has taken excellent care of me. I think, at the time, I paid less than $500 for the two attachments, plus cables, and I picked up a cheap shock mount. I have since gone to a much better shock mount with a nice boom and good wind screen. This piece of gear has made me money. I've used it on my movies, commercial shoots, you name it.

Are there better microphones out there? You bet. Are they

more expensive? Count on it! If I could afford a more expensive mic, I would probably get one, but this Sennheiser has a nice sound, it is adaptable depending on what I need, and has never let me down.

Listen to a microphone, and if you like how it sounds, buy it. Some places will let you demo it if you are a serious customer. We've done that a of couple times, taken a microphone out and recorded some dialog, sound effects, and backgrounds and then played it all back to see how the microphone performed.

To Keep It All Together, You Need To Keep It Separate

When shooting video, you need a separate audio deck. With film, you have to keep audio separate. Film cameras don't record sound.

Most sound heads on video cameras are adequate. You can use them for corporate videos, documentaries (if you are a one-person crew), and on small shoots. I wouldn't use them on a feature.

Film cameras never had sound heads put in them (okay, a couple of cameras were designed to shoot news). For the most part, audio and picture technology was kept separate. I still advocate that today. Audio machines have much better sound heads than cameras. It's all about quality and dynamic range.

I have used non-time-code DATs and everything syncs up just fine. On occasion, they will slip sync a little, but that's a totally fixable problem in the editing room. I have even tried this with film. I took a Sony Datman to Europe with a CP 16 and shot a lot of interviews for a documentary I was doing. The Datman was rock solid, as far as sync. I was impressed. If you're thinking about doing this, shoot a test or two to find out if your gear is compatible.

Angry Filmmaker's note: Video camera companies don't really give a shit about sound! They put their money into picture quality. Sound is merely an afterthought. If they cared about sound, they wouldn't mount the mics onto the cameras. How the hell can you get good sound from a mic that can't move! Everything has to be from the camera's point of view. Does that mean actors have to shout their lines as they get farther away from the camera? What are these idiots thinking?

There are a lot of small location mixers out there. If you have to buy one, call some location sound people and see what they recommend. You can also ask if they have any equipment they might want to part with. As I said before, sound people are good at keeping their gear in great shape. If I was going to buy something used, I would go to a location recordist before I would try a resale shop.

Cut Me

If you're not going to be editing your own movie, find an editor with their own system.

With editing equipment, if you go with either AVID, or Final Cut Pro, you'll be fine. I have friends that use Adobe Premiere, I-movie or stuff like that. If you have it or can get it for free, then go for it. Remember, I cut my first feature on an "obsolete" D-vision system. It worked great and kept track of all the data and the key numbers. When people laughed at my system, I just told them to fuck themselves. (I seem to say that a lot.)

Angry Filmmaker's note: My friend Brian wants me to remind you that many classic films were cut with no more than a razor blade and a Moviscope. And many more were cut on upright Moviolas. You can't get much cruder than that. It doesn't matter what you're cutting your movie on, it's how the movie is cut that's important. If you know a system well and you can get your hands on it cheap, then get it.

I am an Avid person. I have used their system for years, and it does whatever I need it to do. I think they are great! Just my opinion.

Audio doesn't cut itself

Audio editing software is usually expensive, but there are programs you can download as demos. See how much you can do on a demo. You might surprise yourself. There are some sound programs that are available for free as well. Try those out to see if they can do what you need.

Maybe you can find one of George Lucas's old Edit Droid systems. That thing really bombed! He probably destroyed everything and is denying it ever existed. He should. I heard it was a piece of shit, and I am sure there aren't any pieces left over. Remember, this is the same clown who brought the world *Howard the Duck* and *Willow*. Thanks a lot, George.

Don't always think you have to buy editing stuff new. Check places like eBay to see what's out there. (I've seen editing software still in the box for sale, but beware of stuff like this. It's that old, "If it sounds too good to be true...") Also, go to B&H Photo in New York. They only sell new stuff, but their prices are great. And they ship.

But What If I Don't Know Anyone?

You can also sign up for a film class to get access to the gear or just get to know the equipment room people there. Learn the class schedules, find out when the classes will be shooting and when they're not. You can probably cut a great deal on gear from some film programs between semesters.

If you are new to a town, or new to the business, get to know people. Most places have local filmmaking groups. These can be for industry professionals or amateurs with a dream. It doesn't matter.

Talk to lots of people about your movie and what you're trying to do. Be professional and realistic. The more people you get to know, the more you will be able to find whatever you might need. Lots of film students are hoping to break into the business. They might be able to get good experience on your movie. I think knowing lots of people is sometimes better than money. When you have no money, you need a lot of friends to get something done.

Last Thoughts on Scam - uh, I mean Borrowing

Always borrow if you can. And if you can't borrow, wait until you find someone else and borrow from them. If that doesn't work, put your ego in check, and borrow from someone else. You should try all of this at least 10 more times. If that doesn't work, then beg! Go to a rental house, get on your knees and beg. But don't think of it as begging, think of it as borrowing with a lot more effort put into it.

Your movies are important. Whatever little hard-earned money you have should be spent on more important things than equipment. It should be spent on paying off student loans and credit cards. If those are all paid off, then your money should be put into a retirement fund.

If you really must make a movie, then you should take any money you have and use it to buy more time in pre-production, better sound gear, and food for your crew... All worthwhile investments.

Okay, you've "accumulated" all of your gear, and it has cost you next to nothing to use for the next few weeks. I think it's time we go out and shoot something.

CHAPTER 8:

Let's Just Shoot the Bastard

"Whoa, big fella! Before we actually start shooting there are a few more things you need to do."

The more things you can have lined up ahead of time, the better. Why? Because things are going to start falling apart.

Shooting a movie is not really about shooting, it's about planning. Which most people forget. They are so excited about shooting, they rush through all of the planning without giving it adequate time. I know it's really cool to be on the set, but the more you plan, the more fun it will be on the set. And trust me, that's what you want.

I always do a complete run-through of the script with the entire cast as soon as I have a complete cast. We sit around a table and read the entire script, front to back. It is amazing to hear my words come out of other people's mouths for the first time. I swell up with pride listening to them. It's a feeling I can't describe. You have to experience it.

It's also the first time you experience clunky dialog! You might think that everything you've written sounds great, but there is no more humbling experience than to hear a line you have always liked land with a THUD! And it happens. A lot.

The main thing a run-through should accomplish is to show you where the problems are. You have been over this script so many times, you know it forward and backward. You think you've found all the offending dialog and you've fixed everything. No you haven't.

Listen to what the actors are saying. Are there lines that don't sound right? Do you think, "Hey, nobody really talks like that?" Are there lines that draw laughs that aren't supposed to? Uh-oh.

Don't worry, you have plenty of time to fix this stuff. And that's why you do a run-through. This is the only time you'll hear the entire script all the way through until the first rough cut. You want to find all the problems before, not after the shoot.

Before you start rewriting, start rehearsals. Listen to some of those clunky lines again. Maybe it was just a first reaction and the line is okay. Maybe the actor wasn't saying it correctly? Listen to it a few more times, then start working with the actors on it. There's plenty of time to rewrite. You weren't planning on sleeping any time soon, were you?

Hitchcock used to refer to actors as cattle. In my opinion, actors are your greatest asset. Good actors can tell you what's working and what's not by listening to them.

When we were doing *The Gas Cafe*, Bill Ray was having real problems with his character. I was asking him to do things that didn't make sense to him. I wanted him cold and aloof, especially in the beginning, when no one knew who he was. When he talked, it was directed at no one. He wasn't allowed to engage any of the other actors one on one.

This was very hard for him. He was used to working with other actors and wanted to be able to use them to bounce off of. In this movie, that wouldn't happen until much later in the script. It wasn't until we were on the set and he saw how I was filming him, that he finally understood what I was going for. I watched his character spring to life that first night of shooting.

Was this a shortcoming as a director not being able to communicate with him in rehearsals? Perhaps. The important thing was I stuck to my guns in a way that didn't alienate Bill. He eventually saw what I wanted. Remember, making a movie is different from doing theater. If you have actors who have been doing a lot of theater, you have to work a little harder to get them to understand the differences.

There were many days in rehearsal when it wasn't easy. Some days there was quite a bit of tension. Ultimately, Bill's performance is one of the best I've ever gotten. My hat is also off to him for sticking with it until he finally found a way into the character.

Let your actors work their own way. They all work differently. Don Alder, who's been in all of my films, asks a million questions starting from the first day. He doesn't let up until the last day of shooting. He's always questioning his character, and me. There are times when it drives me crazy, but I know this is his way of working.

The actors and the director need to work as one. As the director, you need to listen to your actors. The good ones are doing everything they can to breathe life into the characters you've created. Support them! If you don't, well, let's just say many a good story has been hurt by bad performances. And that's not always the fault of the actors.

Put your ego aside. If an actor wants to change a line, or two, listen. They have to sell it. I always tell my actors the lines of dialog I write are guides. If the lines sound right when you say them, then go for it. If they don't, make changes. If they say, "It'll come out a lot more natural if I say this," that's what you want, a natural-sounding performance.

This is not improv! We work together changing lines before we are on the set! It is the intent of the line that's important, not necessarily the actual wording. As long as I get the same result from a line, a little changing of the words doesn't bother me.

There was a scene in *Birddog* I knew had to be completely rewritten. It read long and boring, but it contained lots of facts I needed to get out so the story would make sense. This is where I learned the power of good acting. I took this scene into rehearsal. The actor who had most of the lines was only in the movie for this one scene. He had to supply a lot of important background information.

I foolishly said, "Let's read through this and then figure out what to cut and where to punch this up." The main character was in agreement, but I noticed that the actor whose lines these were didn't say anything. We started going through the scene and I suddenly found myself lost in his performance. He took what I thought were awkward lines and a ton of facts, and made them all belong to him. It was amazing! At the end of the scene the main actor and I looked at each other totally blown away. This guy did some amazing stuff with a scene I thought needed lots of work.

We did the scene again because I didn't trust what I was hearing. It was just as good if not better. Then we talked and I found out that this actor had first-hand experience with what he was saying. It was even in the same context as the movie. He used that experience. He took my words, made them his own, and

elevated the scene. I am still amazed when I watch that scene.
We stopped rehearsing it after two run throughs because
I wanted to save his performance for the camera.

Remember, you don't know everything! I relearned that day, if
you have really good actors, they can read the phone book and
make it interesting. But, if that's the case, how do we explain
the wooden performances from good actors in the Star Wars
films? I know I am probably picking on George too much.
Don't worry, he's a big guy, he can take it.

You're getting to the end of rehearsing, and guess what? Some
of your actors are having problems with their characters. This is
where you need to have the patience of Job. In some instances,
your actors are right. In others, they just want more screen time.
You get to decide what is really going on.

Angry Filmmaker's note: The easiest way to tell an amateur
filmmaker is to look at the cast. Is everyone in the movie about
the same age as the filmmaker? Do they look like they are
probably friends with of filmmaker? Write the material and cast
a wide range of actors, especially age-wise. The more diverse
your cast is, the more an audience will think they're watching a
"real" movie. If people think they're watching a 20-something
production, they're going to take it less seriously. I'm not saying
you have to write all of your lead actors as different ages, there
can still be 20-somethings in the main roles. I'm saying make
sure that your cast is diverse. Have actors from all walks of life
in various roles. A friend of mine who used to judge film
festivals told me he can usually tell the age of a director by the
cast. It's something to think about.

I know, you're getting a little tired, you're rehearsing like crazy,
and you're doing some rewriting, but you have a lot of other
stuff to do. You need to keep everything moving forward. To

paraphrase Warren Zevon, "You can sleep when you're dead!"

What the Hell Is This?

You'd better be checking your locations. When I write, I usually
have locations in my head, locations I have seen before.
Something about them stood out in my mind or they are places
I know I can get for free. Both of these items are of equal
importance. Don't ever set a scene in a location you know will
be impossible to get. You're just wasting everybody's time.
Sometimes circumstances change and that great location you
had will fall through. Deal with it! Have other ideas.

Visit all your locations at least twice. Why twice? Because
the more you see the location, the better you and your DP can
visualize the scene. You really want to know how to shoot
something in an interesting way that can add to your story.

The first time you go to a location you're going to be thinking
about electrical power, where the sun is at certain times of the
day, a lot of technical things. You might even try to do some
rudimentary blocking.

As rehearsals progress, there will be changes in character and
story, and there might be changes in how you visualize some
things. Maybe a prop or part of a physical location will have
more prominence. You might realize the location presents itself
with visual opportunities you didn't see the first time, or this
location doesn't work as well as another might. Maybe you
want to shoot it at a different time than what you first imagined.
It should be a night scene, not day. If you went to the location
once, you're going to shoot it differently than if you go a second
time. You'll be thinking differently the second time. Trust me
on this one. I am the Angry Filmmaker, why would I lie?
Make sure you have commitments from all your locations in

141

advance! Then have back-ups. I know, if someone says you can use their grandmother's house, it should be fine, right? Wrong! I have lost many locations at the last minute for a variety of reasons. "How many people are on the crew? I thought it was just for a few hours. They want to move what?"

When people realize what a pain in the ass it is to have a crew shoot at their house, things change. I can't blame them, especially if you're not paying them. Who needs it! I have shot many scenes in my own house because of locations falling through. I hate it, and say "Never again."

On *Birddog*, I had to live with my girlfriend for a few days because my house was so trashed, and we weren't getting along well, at that point. I had tons of pressure both on and off the set, and I had no place to go home to. It was not a good situation. Your own house should be a back-up location, but only if you need it.

Why you will be screwed, and like it: Insurance

By the way, are you insured? You'd better be! But shop around. Talk to a few people. Remember, most insurance agents or brokers get a commission based on your premium. That's how they make their money. The larger the premium, the larger the commission. And these people are bastards anyway. They'll try to sell you tons of stuff you don't need, and if you do make a claim, they'll fight you all the way. Remember *Stolen Toyota*.

You need to have insurance because locations, if they're smart, will require an insurance certificate. So will equipment rental houses, if you have to rent. If you're "borrowing" gear, you'd better have insurance. There's nothing worse than borrowing gear and breaking it. You break it, you better fix it!
I know what you're saying, "Nothing ever happens on my

shoots." I had a PA bounce a rental van off a wall, another one put her car in a ditch, and I actually had an actor almost die on my set. So don't give me that "nothing ever happens on my shoots" bullshit!

This actor had a heart problem and had forgotten his medication. He got really sick and then started to freak out, which made things worse. My makeup person stayed with him and kept him calm by talking to him. We got a hold of his son who showed up a while later with his medication. The son stayed on the set for awhile, but the actor told him to go. Naturally, after he left, we had more problems. I finally had the producer and the associate producer drive him home where he could rest. Everything turned out fine, but I was really sweating it. In addition to being one of my actors, he was a good friend.

The worst thing that can happen on a set is that someone gets hurt. Safety is a huge concern. You know what your mom always said, "It's all fun and games until someone gets his eye poked out." You can be as flip and naive as you want, until you meet someone who has lost an eye. Protect yourself, protect and respect your crew. GET INSURANCE!

On *Kicking Bird*, we had a lot of fight scenes, so we had a stunt coordinator. He was a great guy who knew his stuff. Besides a few scrapes and scratches, no one got hurt!

In addition to getting actors to sign releases, get them to fill out a little form that has family phone numbers in case of emergency. And always keep a first-aid kit on the set. That's something we've used a lot.

The moral of this story?

I'm afraid you're going to need insurance, especially if you own anything. If you mess something up, someone will want to sue you and there goes your house, car, dog, or whatever. Just pay the insurance bastards. Then hire a lawyer to make sure if anything happens, the lawyer will stay on the insurance pricks. I'm not much of a fan of insurance guys, but there are good ones (or so I've heard), you just have to hunt.

Everything Breaks, Not Just Your Heart

If you're borrowing a camera, do you have a back-up?

If you're renting, it's up to the people you're renting from to make sure your gear works. You need to check it out ahead of time. Like I said earlier, shoot a test. It doesn't matter if it's film or tape. Test the camera and the lenses before the shoot. Make sure the lenses are good and everything's in focus. Shoot a grid, lighting tests, all of it. It's better to find out something isn't working before you start shooting, rather than the first day on the set. You're going to be crazy on the first day of the shoot anyway, don't add to it.

Check ALL of your gear ahead of time, and make sure, if you're "borrowing," that you have back-ups. Why? Because sometimes, even a good friend, if they get a paying gig with their gear, they're going to bail on you. And they should. They're helping you make your dream come true, but they also have a mortgage, rent, car payment, alimony, or whatever. They need to make money like all of us.

If someone gets a gig with their gear, it's going to be tense, but don't be an asshole about it. Have a back-up plan already in place and go grab another camera, lights, sound gear, whatever. You don't want your crew to hear you bad-mouth someone or piss and moan about "how they promised." Just deal with it and keep shooting. Your cast and crew will respect you a lot more if you just deal with it.

They Were Expendable

During this period when you're still rehearsing, don't be afraid to replace an actor. If they're not getting it, or you think there's going to be trouble later on, get rid of them. Do it in a nice way, but be firm. This is your last chance to make a change before you start shooting. If you have a bad feeling about anyone, cast or crew, make a change. It'll only get worse if you don't.

If you find yourself having conversations with others about problems you're having with someone, do something about it. You have only one chance to get this casting thing right before you commit to shooting.

This goes for the crew as well. If you and the DP are having lots of disagreements, think hard before you proceed. This is someone you're going to be working very closely with for the next few weeks. If the chemistry is not great now, it's probably not going to get any better. It's also better to have some candid discussions now, and part ways before you start working, than to have a lot of tension on the set. Bite the bullet, and remember you're doing it for the good of the project. Your project.

My buddy Brian had to fire a DP once who had his own gear. This had a double impact. You can't fire someone and say, "By the way, can we still use your gear, for free?" It doesn't work that way. You need to find a new DP, sound, or whatever, and replace the gear. If you need to fire someone as important as the DP, check with the other "above the line" folks. If you have their support on this issue, it'll make it easier. It'll also look better to the cast and crew. It won't seem like you are a prima donna who couldn't get along with one person, so they were sacked. It'll look like it was a parting of the ways, by consensus.

145

EVERYONE Wants to Direct

DPs can be a special problem because so many of them "really want to direct." Having someone else on your crew who wants to direct doesn't have to be a problem. We are at a point where everyone thinks they are a director, from the PAs all the way up to the DP, including some of the actors. That's fine as long as everyone realizes on this movie, there is only one director, and that's you!

A Film Crew is Not a Democracy

If other people start telling you what you should be doing on the set, get rid of them! They will talk to others about how you don't know what you are doing, and other crew members might start to wonder as well. As the director, you're in charge of all things creative. Everyone needs to defer to you.

The producer is in charge of financial matters, as it relates to the shoot, and they usually are the ones who have to do the firing. The producer and the director have to work together, but they are in charge of different areas.

The DP shouldn't be talking to the producer about problems they are having with the director. They can, however, talk to the producer about financial issues having to do with the camera department.

There is a clear chain of command on a set, and it should be followed.

The Director is an Asshole

Sometimes, you're the problem. It's you, as the filmmaker, that's an asshole and not listening to others. I know, I know, you're fucking brilliant -- no way it could be you. Remember what George Carlin always said, "Why is it that EVERYONE ELSE drives like an asshole?"

You have to be able to see that, and fire yourself. I don't mean actually fire yourself. Fire the asshole you've become. Mend bridges where necessary, and get a new attitude! Your cast and crew are here to help you, or at least they should be. So take a break, drop back, figure what needs to get done, and then go from there.

People Who Refer to Themselves as "Creatives" Usually Aren't

Angry Filmmaker's note: Why is it that people in the commercial business refer to themselves as "Creatives." They are the least creative people I've ever met. They're just trying to sell shit! The only thing they're doing that's creative is getting people to part with their money. Both consumers and clients. They make professionals do things over and over again until "they get it right," when in reality, they don't know what they want. They cover something from every conceivable angle, performance, or whatever. Then they go into an editing room and mess with it until they get something that's usable, I mean, perfect. Give me a fucking break! With the amount of money that these people waste, anyone could make a 30-second commercial. It takes a lot more creativity to make a feature with no money then to make a 30-second sales pitch with tons of money. Go figure. But I digress.

Where were we? Oh yeah. You were going to do an attitude adjustment and get back to work. At this stage you need to see the whole movie coming together in your head. I start visualizing it while I'm writing. By the time I get to this point, I know my movie inside and out.

I read somewhere it was at this point that Hitchcock always got bored. He was so organized and had everything so thoroughly story boarded that the actual act of shooting was boring to him. He had already made the movie in his head and on paper. Now he just had to shoot the damn thing and let the editor piece it together exactly as he had planned it.

Unlike Hitchcock, for me, the fun is just getting started. I love being on the set, and the act of shooting is one of the all-time greatest acts of aggression that I can imagine.

So let's get going.

CHAPTER 9:

On The Set

"There is no way in Hell we'll get all this done today."

You've made it! You're on the set. It's your first day. You're excited, but wait! There's a problem, and everyone's staring at you waiting for the answer.

Just remember, on your first day of shooting, everything takes longer than planned. You will get done half of what you scheduled. Don't panic! Don't lose control! It's all going to be okay. It just takes time to work the bugs out.

For those of you who have seen *Living In Oblivion* (the best movie about making a movie), there is a wonderful scene that's repeated throughout of various crew members sniffing the milk container on the craft services table after they've poured themselves a cup of coffee. Everyone makes a face, puts it down and walks away. That's just one little jab pointed at all those filmmakers who don't take care of their crew in the simplest ways.

Living In Oblivion is a great film that should be required viewing for anyone who wants to make a feature. You will laugh at the stuff that goes on, but just about every low-budget shoot that I have ever worked on had at least one of those elements happen. I think the movie is a documentary. It's a good way to avoid pitfalls. I walked out of the theater feeling like I had worked with half of the crew portrayed in the movie. If you want to make movies, see it.

Angry Filmmaker's note: Remember what I said earlier about not making movies about movies? *Living In Oblivion* is the exception. It is so good that, as far as I'm concerned, it's been done. No one can do it better, so don't even try. There are already lots of movies about the film business: *The Player, Day of the Locust*, the list goes on and on. Make a movie about something else and leave the parodies to the professionals.

Oh Boy! Here We Go!

When you plan your first day's shoot, give yourself less to do than on the rest of the schedule. Why? Because you have a new crew that is going to have to learn to work together. You have actors who are still getting used to their characters. And Murphy's Law is going to be working overtime to make sure even the simplest things don't come together easily.

Welcome to the World of Independent Filmmaking

As the filmmaker, you are in charge. The producer always thinks they're in charge, but that's not true, unless, of course, you're the producer as well. If you are the producer, make sure you have a really good associate producer or production manager. Someone needs to keep other parts of the schedule running smoothly because no matter how good you think you are, or how big your ego is, you can't do it all.

I don't recommend being your own producer if you are the

director as well. It's not an easy thing to pull off, especially if this is your first or second time directing. On all of my features, I have worked with a producer, Nicola Silverstone. She handles a lot of the things I don't have time to handle. Because I do have a big ego and I am the one that puts most of my movies together, I take a producing credit as well. I do a lot of producing, just not all of it.

The Agony and The Ego

Let's learn about ego, right now. Egos seem to present themselves when you get onto the set.

You are going to have disagreements, people aren't going to listen to you, actors will be late or unprepared, and stuff is going to get set up wrong. And this is with a good crew. When you're using first-timers in some positions, oh my God!

Here's a couple of things to keep in mind.

Don't ever lose your temper. Let me repeat that. **DON'T EVER LOSE YOUR TEMPER!**

Other people can get upset, but you can't. Once you do, the whole day is screwed and possibly the entire shoot. People are working their asses off for you. It's not the script, the food, or anything else. It's you! There is something about you they like and are willing to give up their time to work with you. If you lose your temper, and start yelling, calling people names, they are going to lose all respect for you. If they don't respect you, they won't work hard. They might not even show up the following day.

Angry Filmmaker's note: There are some commercial directors who have reputations when it comes to their tempers, but as we all know, commercial directors aren't real directors anyway. (I'm talking about you, Joe!) They want to be directing features, and a few of them have made the switch, but for the most part, they're high-priced whores who are just trying to sell stuff we don't need. There are also a few feature directors with legendary tempers, but most of them haven't had a hit in years and are living off past glories. Can anyone say William Friedkin?

Stay cool under fire at all times. If you need to get pissed, walk away from the set, walk around the block, kick a dog or small child, whatever it takes. Regain your composure and come back.

Make the Noise Stop!

The most important thing is to have a quiet set. I mean quiet even when you're not shooting. My hearing is not what it once was, too much sound editing, sound mixing and loud rock and roll. If I'm in a place with lots of people, like a bar, a restaurant, or even a party, I have difficulty distinguishing voices from the background. If you aren't facing me so I can see your mouth move, I really can't hear you.

As a rule, my DP and I always say at the beginning of each shoot that everyone needs to talk only when necessary. Otherwise, I can't hear what the DP is saying and that will slow the whole process down. Since I've been working with a lot of the same people for years, everyone understands this and I have one of the quieter sets. I think it makes us work more efficiently.

I'm not saying that everyone has to work in silence; it's the unnecessary talking I don't like. If you want to tell someone how hammered you got last night, go over to the craft services table and talk during a break. Trust me, there will be lots of breaks during any shoot day. When you're on the set, restrict your talking to what is going on. Everyone will appreciate it and more work will get done.

There is also a chain of command, on the set, that needs to be respected. I know it sounds elitist, but not everyone can talk to the director. If you work on the lighting crew and there's a problem, tell the gaffer. If you work on the camera crew and you think there's a problem, tell the DP. The gaffer will relay problems to the DP, and if the two of them can't figure it out, then they'll go to the director.

As the filmmaker, I am concerned with every little detail. The reason we have crews with a hierarchy is so the people I've put around me can solve problems. If nothing else, those people can be my filter and decide what is important for me to know, and what can be fixed without my knowledge. I trust them to make the right decisions, and when they do have a question, then we talk and figure it out.

If you're a PA, fresh out of school, and this is one of your first gigs, let me give you some advice.

The Director Doesn't Give a Shit About Your Opinion!

It's harsh, but true. When we were making *Birddog*, there was a PA who asked me why I was doing a particular shot from a particular angle. It didn't really look that good to her. As politely as I could, I told her that her input was not needed, especially since this was her first day on the shoot and we had been shooting for two weeks. I tried to remind her what her role was, what mine was, and she needed to take care of her job, and let me do mine. Then I spoke to the AD and said to keep her the hell away from me! Trust me, you have enough on your mind, and unsolicited input from a young PA isn't what you need.

I mean, does the waterboy talk to the quarterback about his

passing? Does an intern talk to a surgeon about an operation? Does an alcoholic talk to the bartender about... You get what I mean.

Light Me Up

Remember what I said about lighting an entire set before you start shooting? Well, it's time to think about that now. Look at your scene, your shot list and the location. How much time can you save by lighting the whole set all at once?

It will take longer to do in the beginning, but once you start shooting you will be able to change angles much quicker. Your actors can work more efficiently, because there is less time between setups. It shouldn't take them as long to get into character. One hopes, anyway.

I learned this trick from Jean Yves Escoffier, the DP on *Good Will Hunting*. He told me he did this on all his movies. It makes sense. He was an amazing fellow and a terrific DP. Look him up on IMDB and check out some of his other movies. He passed away too young.

Just because you're shooting video doesn't mean you don't have to light! And don't use that bullshit excuse, "I'm doing this guerrilla-style." I don't care what you think you're doing, light the damn actors! When I see movies that have been done without any lighting, I'm rarely impressed. Did you know we even light documentaries on video? Take the time and light your set.

If you're shooting tape, light it as if it were film. When people see something shot on video and comment on how good it looks, it's probably because it was well lit. I would rather take an extra hour at the beginning of each scene to light the whole

154

thing than to light just what I need for the master, then relight for each medium shot or close-up. The lighting of each individual shot can eat up hours on the set when you add it all together. When you think about it, lighting the whole set just makes even more sense if you are using the entire set.

When I wrote *Kicking Bird*, I designed it to be shot quickly with a minimum of hassles. Most scenes are shot outdoors with minimal lighting, using bounce cards and reflectors.

I always like to ask the question in my seminars after people have seen *Kicking Bird:* "Why did I use cross country as the sport the main character ends up doing? Why not one of the other running events?"

Cross country is one of the few high school running sports that takes place in the fall. The weather (in Oregon anyway) is usually bad, and cross country teams are small! There can be three, four or eight people on a team. There are no other track and field events during the cross country season and the runners don't run on a track!

In spring running events are usually held on a track, along with shot put, long jump, pole vault, etc. So you have fairly large teams in a single place. You also have spectators! Since I have no money, I don't want to put together a bunch of other events for the background. I don't want to deal with, and can't afford, a bunch of extras. Also, running around a track is BORING!

By doing cross country, I have small teams, and they only start and end on a track. If they are running around a city or through the woods, you don't need a lot of spectators, so my crowds are much smaller. I mean, come on, if you are going to watch a cross country race, all you really get to see is the start and the finish. I can also shoot running shots in interesting locations, quickly and with no permits.

When people see the movie, they aren't asking where the big track and field scenes are. Where are the crowds? There aren't any. People know that without being told.

By shooting a fall sport, I don't have to worry about the weather. It can rain or be sunny, it can even snow. It doesn't matter. If I'm shooting a spring sport, I need to have some sunshine. That's what an audience expects.

By having the characters as runners, I can shoot a lot of running footage documentary-style and NOT have to worry about lighting or reflectors. The sky is overcast and the camera is bouncing a bit, but with some decent music and some fast editing, the audience will overlook shots that may or may not be pretty.

Angry Filmmakers note: Using cross country and running as a metaphor for Martin's life was also fitting. He's running away from his horrible life, and he's going to have to run a long way to get away from the things holding him back. What is he running to? He doesn't know, he just knows he needs to keep running. Maybe it's the running itself that will finally be his escape.

We worked hard to set up interesting shots, and by being able to shoot anywhere we wanted, we could pick and choose our locations and have some nice visuals. The visuals added to the story. Martin's team, from the poor side of town, runs through beat-up neighborhoods and vacant lots, not lush green running trails like suburban schools have. From these visuals you know that this team, and their school, is in a poor neighborhood. That helps the story and helps create the background of the characters.

Angry Filmmaker's note: When you're doing a lot of work

outdoors in the cold, have lots of warm drinks available for the cast and crew. For the runners we always had lots of water. We had coats and blankets to keep them warm between takes.

Try to keep your shooting times to a reasonable length. Keep your days to ten hours. Sometimes it works, sometimes it doesn't. Sometimes you need to shoot longer, depending on how the day has gone, or you need to wrap a location. When these issues arise, talk to your crew. Tell them you're going to need another hour or two to wrap the location, the scene or whatever. Make sure that's okay with everyone.

What? Ask the crew members if it's okay to work longer? You're goddamn right! You're going to work overtime anyway, but asking them if it's okay is showing respect for them and their time.

I've never been on a shoot where people said, "No, let's just call it a day." It doesn't work that way. People will stay and work as late as you need them. And if you ask them first, they'll work harder so that they can go home. Sometimes people will have other commitments and can't stay longer. That's okay too. Remember, you're not paying these people. If you are, you're not paying them well. If a crew member has something they need to do, let them go as long as someone else can cover for them. Trust me, everyone involved will appreciate it.

I was doing a paying gig and one of my main actors was also doing a play in the evenings. We hit a point where we were going to have trouble finishing on time. I knew this actor had to leave soon. I checked with the rest of the cast and crew and we made sure that everyone knew he had to leave. Then I changed the schedule for the rest of the afternoon so that we could get all of his shots done first so he could leave.

We ended up working an hour longer than originally scheduled, the actor got his stuff done and barely made his evening performance. Everyone appreciated what we needed to do, to get him out on time, and no one pissed and moaned about working overtime. I'm not sure, but I think no one billed me for overtime either. I like to think that was because I asked everyone first about the schedule change and they knew why. It's great to work with real professionals.

Use this same method if a particular shot is going longer and you need to break for lunch. There's usually a set amount of hours you can work before you have to feed people. Even on independent films. It's around five hours. There are times when the lunch break is approaching and you need to get one last shot. I always check with the crew and they are usually okay with it, I also release anyone who isn't necessary to the shot and let them go eat. I am left with a smaller crew which always works out.

Remember, it's that show of respect that's really important. If your cast and crew don't respect you, but just like you (respect is a bit more important), then they are not going to go that extra mile that's going to make your movie better.

Angry Filmmaker's note: I worked on a video shoot with another director. We split up the project and I directed some days, he directed other days, all with the same cast and crew. I'll be nice and say the other director was not a people person. He never bothered to learn crew member's names. Instead he called them by their positions, and had a nasty temper. By the time I came back to finish the last part of the show, the crew absolutely despised him. The clients weren't too wild about him either.

He consistently worked the crew longer than the normal 10-hour days and we were charged overtime by the crew for every one of those days. I had a lot of work to finish on the final day and I called the crew together, informing them we were probably going to run overtime and hoped that was okay. I also said I would be buying drinks and appetizers at the bar down the street after we wrapped to thank everyone for their hard work. We went almost two hours overtime, including the wrap. We finished the day with food and drink, and I don't recall anyone billing us for overtime for that particular day.

The Agony and the Ecstasy: Crew Romances

Let's take a moment to talk about crew romances. They always happen. Sometimes they work, sometimes they can be very disruptive. Watch out for them. I'm not talking about hiring two people who are already a couple. That has its own set of problems. I'm talking about the hook-ups that happen on the crew while you're shooting. Yes, friends, it happens all the time.

Why You Need to be a Monk -- Or Get Laid on Your Own Time

If you're the director, and you get involved with a cast or crew member during production, YOU'RE AN IDIOT! Why? Because you're in charge, moron. If you start seeing someone who works for you, things are going to change.

Suppose you're dating the assistant camera person and he/she is bad-mouthing the DP. Suddenly, you're not so confident with the DP anymore. And they feel that. They can either bend over backwards to accommodate the AC so you won't get pissed, or they'll treat them like shit because they're pissed off by the whole situation. Either way, they're not concentrating on the movie. Your loss.

If you, as the filmmaker, hook up with a cast member, YOU'RE AN EVEN BIGGER IDIOT! Suddenly one person is going to

159

be getting more close-ups. Maybe the lead actor starts making more demands, and you say, "That's okay, she's an artist and she needs it; even though I can't afford it, we can do that."

You have just lost control of your movie, shithead! I'm not saying it isn't true love, mind you, but it's not! It's manipulation. These people are actors, get it? The odds are, it ain't gonna last, and worse, it's going to affect your movie. As a director, don't do it. You've worked too hard to get to this point. Make your damn movie and screw up about your personal life later.

I have seen crew members hook up with each other. Sometimes it works, and sometimes they both show up on the set pissed off at each other. It makes everyone else uncomfortable. Tension on the set -- not good.

When actors hook up with that can also be a problem. Some actors have affairs during the production and when their part is over, they drift away and go back to their normal lives and other relationships. I don't know how they do it, but they do.

When an actor and a crew person hook up, it gets weird. I had that happen once. A crew person hooked up with one of my leads. She turned his world upside down, then dumped him. It was a little tough on his head, and it really pissed me off. They would talk together between takes, when she should have been working. I told the production manager to find more for that crew person to do. NOW!

That's not to say I haven't been tempted myself. But I would never put my movie in jeopardy by acting on that attraction. After the wrap? That's different. It usually doesn't happen either, because there's nothing to be gained by a romance at that point, as far as some people are concerned.

You Can't Be Everywhere - - Leave the Crew Alone!

When I talk about respect for the cast and crew, I'm also talking about respect for their craft. You have had discussions with the various department heads, you've done your shot lists, lighting diagrams, story boards, or whatever it is you use. Now let those department heads run with the ball.

Don't micro-manage. You hired them for a reason. Trust them. I'm not saying don't have discussions on the set. You will make changes. Just don't stand behind everyone telling them how to do their job. It pisses them off and you have more important things to do than to make sure the donuts are in the right place on the counter. Leave that to the art department and the DP.

Don't Embarrass the Actors

On the set, the director's main focus should be the actors. You have hired the crew and are letting them do their jobs. Now really concentrate on the actors. Make sure they have the tools they need to do the scene. Too many directors get all hung up on the shot and other technical aspects of the scene, and not with the actors. The actors' performances are much more important, at this point, than an additional light, a different prop on the counter, or anything else.

After a take, if you want performance changes, go up to them and quietly talk to them. Don't shout it out. The discussions you have with any actor to get a performance should be private. I see commercial directors and amateurs shout out directions to actors from a distance. They treat the cast like just another prop. They could get better performances if they took a little extra time and showed the actors some respect.

As the director, you are going to want that actor to dig down deep inside and to go to a place where they can make that character become whole for a particular scene. Give them that opportunity. What they have to do and where they have to go within themselves is no one's business. Keep your conversations private.

The PAs, camera crew, or anyone else don't need to hear you talk to actors about their motivation. It can be embarrassing, depending on what you two are using for motivation. If they start feeling self conscious, their performance is going to suffer. The actor's relationship with you is going to suffer as well, and it'll be tougher to get those kinds of performances from them in the future.

My AD and DP always keep the crew quiet and ready when I have conversations with an actor. As soon as we are done, I take my place near the camera and have the actor tell me when he or she is ready, and we do it again.

When I say "cut" after a shot, I usually look at both the DP and the sound recordist and wait for them to assure me that everything on that take was right. That is unless I didn't like the performance or I saw something that I didn't like.

My DP and I work so closely, many times when I felt there was a problem with an actor's performance and wanted to do it again for my own weird reasons (which I don't want to explain because I can see the actor is getting frustrated), he'll take the bullet and ask to do it again for camera. This makes the actor feel as if it wasn't their fault (it is, but you don't want them to know that), and they usually do a better job next time. My DP is always great about reassuring the actors that they're doing a good job.

I also need to hear from the sound recordist whether the take was clean. That's really important to me. If there are sound problems such as, airplanes, cars, screaming, gunshots, or whatever, I want to do it again, if I can. I don't want to have to fix sound in post. I know what the pitfalls are, but we'll be getting to that shortly. If there are problems with sound, do it again. It's safer, smarter, and ultimately more cost efficient.

I Hate Video Monitors On My Set

I hate to look at playback on the set. That means everyone wants to look, including the actors, and that's not necessarily a good thing.

There was a story years ago when they were making the film *Priscilla, Queen of the Desert,* that Terrance Stamp, who was playing an over-the-top drag queen, refused to watch any dailies. He was afraid if he saw himself , he would get freaked out by his performance. He would become self-conscious and try to ratchet it back. He felt it was better not to see anything and trust the director and his own skills. It's an amazing performance. Check it out.

In my mind, the problem with looking at playback on the set is that you're letting everyone see what you're doing on a small monitor (usually black & white). You're looking at one take, and that can have an effect on everything if you're not careful.

A crew member could say something accidentally or unconsciously (and if they do on my set, then they will be unconscious) that can really bother an actor, and then the actor has trouble concentrating. The actor might not be wild about his performance and start making changes based on what they are hearing the crew say.

A tiny black & white monitor is not going to make the lighting or the makeup look its best. Why monitors are even allowed on set is still a mystery to me. Remember all those classic movies we were talking about earlier? No monitors on the set.

Monitors help the script supervisor, but as far as I'm concerned, that's all they're good for. I hate them!

When I am directing, I stand right next to the camera, as close as I can to the actors. I want to "feel" their performances. I have been told by cast and crew that when I am directing, I am mouthing the words and feeling every insult and every punch my characters receive. I know, I created them from parts of my own life. When I am directing, I am every character in the movie. I physically feel all their pain and all their joy as we shoot. Directing is exhausting for me. It has to be, otherwise I couldn't get the performances I get.

You can't feel performances looking at a small black & white monitor. Monitors should only be used if you have a complicated moving shot. But even with those, I am standing right next to my DP as he is moving and I ask him at the end whether the shot felt good. If he thinks it did, and I like the acting, we move on. Monitors are a crutch for insecure directors.

Angry Filmmaker's note: It is on commercials that monitors get the most use. The ad agency "creatives" (remember them?) sit around the monitors and second-guess everything the director is doing. On commercials, these people rarely know what the fuck they're doing besides wasting tons of clients' money. I did those for a while; that's not filmmaking.

Tips of the Trade

Fritz Lang always used to be the first one on the set and the last one to go home at night. He led by example. He said if the crew saw he was there before them and there when they left, they really couldn't complain about the hours. I always try to be the first there, but the crew usually tells me to go home while they're wrapping. They know how hard I work.

Some directors are real partiers. If that is your style, fine. Personally, I like to be on my "A" game while I'm shooting. Hangovers get worse the older you get. I might have a beer or two at the end of a day, but get hammered? You've got to be kidding!

I may be organized, but I am always alert when it comes to something that wasn't planned. I've spent enough years doing this to realize sometimes things happen that weren't planned. Always be aware, and if it is better than what was planned, run with it.

I always wait a beat before saying "Action" and "Cut." I do that for sound. I want a moment or two of silence on each take to use in sound post-production, in case I have room tone holes I need to fill when we're editing.

After each take I tell the script supervisor which parts of the take I like best and why. They should write it down so you have notes when you're editing.

Always make sure that your location sound people keep logs just like the camera department. I want a separate sheet for each audio roll because I want to know what scenes and takes are on what sound roll and if they got any additional audio they think can come in handy while editing.

Make sure your wardrobe people take a digital still of each actor in each costume change for the entire movie. They should write on that photo what day or scene that outfit is to be used in. This should been done ahead of time. A complete set of photos should be on location so that there is no confusion about wardrobe for any scene.

If you are shooting in bad weather, always keep an extra set of dry clothes and shoes in your car for the drive home. There is nothing worse than wearing wet clothes at the end of the day. That's when people get sick.

So let's shoot this thing, we're burning daylight here. Go!

CHAPTER 10:

What do you mean, "coverage?"

"If you can't solve it, dissolve it."

You finally got your movie shot. Congratulations!

A Different View of Hell

It's editing time. That time when you realize everything you missed when you were on the set. I know, you could have sworn you had gotten close-ups on that scene, but they're not there. I guess you were in a hurry. Now what?

The editing process can be the most painful, or the most fun depending on your attitude and how well organized you are. There are two schools of thought here. One, we're going to do a rough cut, figure out what we need, then go out and reshoot.

Or, this is what we have, so let's make the best of it.

Personally, I'm a fan of the second one. If you need to go back out and shoot, I guess you haven't been paying attention to the earlier parts of this book. Way to fly, Orville!

Here are my reasons not to reshoot: It costs money. You have to get your cast and crew back together again. The actors have to get excited all over again. It costs money. You have to try to make the new stuff match with the old stuff. It costs money. Your locations might have changed, or be gone (torn down). You might not be able to get locations again (the owners hate you). It costs money. All those props you used have been returned. It costs money. Some actors have left town or the business. And, it costs money.

I have been trying to tell you how to do things cheaply and efficiently so you wouldn't have this problem, and you weren't listening. Maybe you should just put this book away; obviously, you're not taking this seriously.

Sometimes you do run into major problems and you have to go out and do pickups. These should all be inserts, the kind you and the DP can get by yourselves, an establishing shot of a building, a close-up on a book or letter, footsteps, the Cavalry coming over the hill to save the wagon train. Stuff like that.

I told you about re-shooting on **The Gas Cafe**. It was hard to get the excitement back up, schedule the crew, the locations, everything. And that wasn't for a reshoot, it was just to finish the movie after principal photography was over. Imagine waiting six months and then trying to get people and locations back. Avoid reshooting at all costs.

If You Must Go Back

With *Birddog*, after we edited the film, we found places where putting in a few new inserts would help the story's flow. Randy and I went out and shot them in one day.

The only problem we had was the train shot in front of the bar.

We were told the train would go by around 11 p.m. So we got there early and waited. Kathy Peterson, one of the owners of The Dockside, came down and turned on all the lights so it would look like it was open. Then we set up across the street and waited. We sat there for five hours. We called the train people and they kept assuring us it was going to be coming by, soon. They lied! It was around 4 a.m. when that damn thing finally crossed in front of the bar. We only had one chance to shoot it. We got it and went home and crashed. It was a really long day thanks to our friends at the railroad.

With *Kicking Bird*, reshooting wasn't an option. We never picked up anything. I honestly can't think of anything I wanted to go pick up. When we were done shooting, we were done shooting.

Log and Load

Let's look at your footage. If you had a good script supervisor, there's a lot of stuff you don't need to input into your editing system. Look at their notes, then just input circled takes. At this point, don't waste your time looking at the bad takes. Don't worry, you'll end up going through them later, when you're looking for part of a shot you can use to cut between two other angles because your action doesn't match.

Anyone who inputs everything from the shoot either has tons of hard-drive space or doesn't know much about editing.

If your script notes suck, you'll have to watch the material as you're inputting it. If you see bad takes, delete them. Save space on your hard drives. Remember, the more crap you have in your system, the slower it works. Plus, you are going to end up going through the bad stuff every time you are looking for something. I know, I have.

Angry Filmmaker's note: Check your firewire drives. Some are designed for picture editing, some are designed for storage. When you're cutting picture, it takes a lot of memory to do this, especially in real time. The connection between your drives and computer has to be fast and stable

I always arrange my editing bins by script day, just like my script breakdown. That way, I put all the footage for a "story" day in one bin and I can refer to my script as I'm editing. For me, it makes it faster and more efficient. Some people arrange their bins by scene; and have a separate bin for each scene. I think that's too many bins. The goal is to make everything simple and easy to find.

Since you were smart enough not to record your audio straight onto the camera, once you get all of your picture input, you need to input the audio. Once again I put the audio into its own bins arranged by "story" day.

I also like to put the audio on a different hard drive than the picture. The computer seems to run more efficiently that way. A long time ago, when drives were smaller and CPUs slower, a video engineer told me to do it that way. It helped the computer process things much quicker. Now, it's just habit. And still a good one, I think.

I use the camera mic to record a reference track while I'm shooting. This is where it's going to come in handy. In film, you always use your slate to match up picture and audio, first frame of the clap on audio, to first frame where the sticks actually hit on film. I use the same method when working in video. If everything is working correctly, your reference audio track will phase with the track off your separate audio recorder. When you play the two tracks together, they should run at exactly the same speed. What you should hear is one track, with a lot of extra background noise from the camera mic.

I always put the camera mic track on audio one and put my good audio on audio two. I leave them both set up that way while I'm editing. I turn off track one so that I can't hear it, but every cut I make on audio two, I make to audio one. That way while I'm editing, I can turn on audio one at any time and use it as a reference to make sure that my audio is still in sync with the picture. There may be easier ways to do this, but this is my way, and so far it's been pretty foolproof.

You need to keep good notes when you're beginning the editing process. Why? Because you are going to be editing for a long time and you want to be able to quickly go back through the bins to find things you didn't think you were going to use. Plus, the way you shot things, you may need to go through different bins to find stuff that's going to save your butt.

Like any part of the filmmaking process, you need to stay neat and organized. It's going to save you time in the long run. The simpler your record-keeping and organization, the more time you have to do the fun creative stuff. Isn't that what we all want? Except for you suffering artist types who want the whole process to torment you so you can walk around and act like the "put upon" artist. It may get you laid, but it's going to cause unnecessary problems in the editing room. Personally, I'm lazy and would rather put out a little extra effort in the beginning so I don't have to pull my hair out later. I'm funny that way.

Whether you're using Avid, Final Cut Pro, or whatever, there is something I've noticed newer editors do that drives me absolutely crazy. They use too many video and audio tracks when they edit. I have seen them spread the material over four or five video tracks, and eight or twelve audio tracks on a first cut! What the hell are you doing?

This is too much unnecessary work. Every time you make an edit on one track, you have to make a change on eight, or nine, or twelve, or more tracks. You'll spend more time keeping everything in sync than actually making creative edits. It slows your computer down because you're using a lot more RAM than you need.

I cut on one video track, at least through the first three or four edits, and try to keep my audio to a minimum of five tracks. I have my reference track, turned off but running, my main dialog is on two, three for overlapping dialog where needed, and music on four and five. If I need to add more tracks, I wait. I don't need to add sound effects yet. Not on a first cut or three. And if I do, I throw one mono effect in on the extra dialog track I'm using only for overlaps.

I cut on one video track. If I need to do a super, an effect, or a title, I wait until I have the whole movie cut at least once. Usually, it's on cut three that I start putting in my visual effects. I can visualize the effects up until that point. Besides, I'm not showing the first couple of cuts to anyone. They are like drafts when I'm writing. You don't show your first attempt because it's too rough.

Angry Filmmaker's note: My first edits are always long. I put in everything, just like I write, because I want to see everything. I want one cut of the movie that has all my options. I know that I can drop some of those options while I'm cutting them, but at this stage it's too soon to tell.

I always watch my first couple rough-cuts by myself and take lots of notes. Then I get out my chain saw and the real editing begins.

The Texas Chainsaw Edit

I cut my features myself. I don't recommend this; it depends on your experience level. I was an editor long before I started directing. I am pretty brutal when it comes to cutting down my own work. I can put my movies together faster than anyone else, but I also feel at this point in my career, that I have a good handle on what I want and how best to put it all together.

I will bring in another editor on occasion, which I did on *Birddog*. I'd taken that movie as far as I could and needed help figuring some things out. Now, I do it all myself.

Just like in the writing stage, I bring in people I trust to watch the movie and get their reaction. I usually do this with my third cut. I write specific questions and have them fill out a form. After the screening, we talk about other things in the movie I may not have covered with the questions.

The questions usually include: What is this movie about? What is your first impression of the movie? What character(s) do you like and why? What character(s) don't you like and why? Were you lost at all during the story? What scene do you like best and why? What scenes bothered you? Did any scene feel too long? Did any scene feel too short? Would you recommend this movie to your friends? Is there anything else you want to tell my about the movie?

I sit in the back at these screenings so I can watch the audience. I learn more about what they like and don't like by listening to them as they watch. Are they laughing in the right place or the wrong place? Are they fidgeting at places? Does something feel too long? After awhile, you can get a good hit on how the audience is feeling just by listening to them. The questionnaires just reinforce those feelings.

I listen to what people have to say, but I also take it with a grain of salt. Like the scripting stage, I'm looking for the same

problems or observations that come from more than one person.
Is there any consistency in people's complaints? If so, I have
a problem.

Remember, when you're looking for feedback on a script or a
rough cut, make sure the people you're showing your work to
don't have their own agenda. Make sure that anything they say
is about you and your project, not about them.

There are certain filmmakers I know who I would never bring
into my rough-cut screenings. I found this out the hard way.
I made a couple of movies and one filmmaker in particular
would just rip my work apart! He would tell me how I failed
and my movie didn't work! I would get really depressed. This
was a filmmaker who was quite respected and he was telling me
my movies were crap.

He always had ways for me to fix them, but what I learned was
that his solutions to my "problems" were always the same. They
would make my movies like his. And we have two absolutely
different styles (besides, he has never made a feature). He is no
longer invited to my rough-cut screenings, and I don't miss his
feedback, which wasn't really feedback. It was all about him.

When possible, I like to put the movie away for a week at this
stage. So I can think about other things and then come back and
try to look at it from a fresh perspective. This never works, but
I'm usually grateful, at this point, for any time away from the
movie. Then it's back to work.

Angry Filmmaker's note: The problem I have is I'm trying to
cut my movies while I'm hustling other work, doing other work,
or just trying to have a life. The editing process takes longer than
I want. It's the reality of being a working filmmaker without a
trust fund. I need to make some sort of living and I'm getting too

old to live on oatmeal. You know what? Filmmaking is hard. Getting through the editing stage is not easy, and you just have to deal with it.

You've Lost That Lovin' Feeling

If you've to put your movie away for awhile, how do you maintain your excitement when you come back? It's YOUR movie, moron. You better still be excited! Seriously, there are times when you don't want to sit down and work on it. You're tired, the sun is out (a rare occurrence in Oregon), or you just want a break. Well, take one! Since no one is paying you, don't force it! I have seen too many people, after six months or longer, who want to hurry up and just finish the movie. I've been guilty of it myself. You're not doing your movie, or the cast and crew, any favors by saying, "I just need to finish this damn thing! I don't care anymore."

Here's that respect thing, again. The best way to show respect to the people who supported you, worked with you, and believed in you, is to finish the movie and make it the best movie possible. This is what separates the professionals from the posers.

The professional will separate themselves from all the shit in their lives and work at the highest level possible to get it done to the best of their ability. The posers will either not finish it, or if they do, you can see they rushed through it. And it won't be that good. Maybe the posers figured out real quick their movie wasn't very good, or as good as they thought it would be and they're embarrassed by it. They want to move on and do something else (plumbing perhaps?), but they feel like they have to finish it. "Gosh, this making a movie is tougher than I thought."

One of the great things I learned in film school was you always finish what you've started. It doesn't matter how bad it is, you made a commitment and you have to see it through. I don't know if USC still teaches that philosophy, but it's really important. You do the best job you can even when the ship is sinking. It doesn't matter. You signed on. I worked on a few student movies and some features that ended up being really bad, but no one on the crew ever quit. You just don't do that.

If you know your movie sucks, finish it for your cast and crew. But, please don't make the rest of us sit through it!

I'll Take Potpourri for $300, Alex

Other thoughts on rough-cut screenings and showing stuff that you're working on to your friends: A lot of people don't understand what a movie looks like when it's "in process," i.e. not completed. I have seen people show friends sequences from their movies out of context and not even close to finished. This never helps a filmmaker.

I know you're excited about your movie and you want to show stuff as soon as you can. If people don't start jumping up and down and say what they've just watched is the greatest thing ever, then you get bummed. What are you thinking, jackass? Of course they're not jumping up and down. It's not finished, it's out of context and they don't have the vision you have.

I don't care how much you think you or your friends know about movies. What many of you learned came through watching the special features and director's commentaries on some DVDs. That doesn't tell you anything. I have watched major movies in rough cut that looked like crap and went on to do great business at the box office. But I knew what work needed to be done to get them ready. Most people don't.

I will NOT look at individual completed scenes from a movie.

They tell me nothing! I would rather look at a really long rough cut of the entire movie, than a couple of scenes that have been cut. To judge a movie, you have to feel its pace, see the whole story. A particular scene could be brilliant! But the scenes around it aren't. I need to see something from start to finish so I can get a feel for the movie and give quality feedback.

I made the mistake, once, of showing a local film critic the first 15 minutes of one of my features while it was still in rough cut. Boy was that stupid! A year later, when I was set to premiere it, he told one of the local art house theater owners that he wasn't going to be reviewing it. He had seen it already and it wasn't very good! He assigned someone else to do it. All he had seen was a 15-minute piece! And there he was telling a theater owner no less it wasn't very good. I wonder who else he told? I will never, ever make that mistake again. I learned my lesson.

Angry Filmmaker's note: How many of you think we use all the sound we record on the set for everything in the movie? The backgrounds? Car-bys? And how many of you think we loop (replace the dialog) 90% of the movie? The truth is, your friends and some film critics don't know shit when it comes to making a movie. Don't show them anything until you at least have a complete rough-cut.

The other thing that drives me nuts is when the camera department comes into look at a cut. I love my DP, but we watch movies differently. He looks at the lighting and the shots, not the story. He kicks himself about how he should have done things differently. He wonders why I didn't use a particular shot that took a long time to set up.

Randy, my DP never asks why I didn't use a particular shot. He's a lot smarter than most DPs. He knows it probably didn't fit in with the scene as a whole. I have sat in on editing sessions where a DP spent quite a bit of time trying to re-cut the movie in his head so the editor could work some favorite shot in. If the shot is too beautiful, too visually interesting, and most of all, stands out from the rest of the stuff around it, GET RID OF IT! It doesn't belong. It draws attention to itself.

After your rough-cut screenings, when you've made all the minor changes you need to, or the major ones if you really did mess up, it's time to start prepping to do the sound and finish this monster.

Stick a Fork In It?

It's up to you whether you finish the edit and pull your master straight off the hard drives. If your picture is compressed on your editing system, or if you shot film and want to go back to a cut film negative, you need to make some decisions to help you finish your movie in the best possible way.

If you've shot film, when they transferred your film to tape, I really hope they made flex files for you. What's a flex file?

Schwarzenegger Does Not Use Flex Files

A flex file is a file that contains the key numbers from the rolls of negative. Each roll has its own set of key numbers. Kodak and Fuji put them on every negative photographically. They are on every roll of film, and when the film is processed, they appear. On 16mm they appear every 20 frames; in 35mm, it's every foot. Negative cutters use them to cut the negative so that it matches your work print in film. If you look on the side of a roll of film, either negative or work print, you will see the numbers. They're located between the sprocket holes.

If you're shooting film, cutting on tape and plan to finish on film, then you need to have these key numbers for the negative cutters down the road. The flex files log the key numbers to correspond with camera roll numbers and time code. You need to remember to load the flex files as you're inputting your shots so the computer has a way of tracking all this information. And remember, key numbers are all different. Two pieces of negative can't have the same numbers. Kodak and Fuji don't do it that way.

Do flex files work? When we shot **Birddog**, I did all of my editing on an old D-Vision system. I can't speak for others, but as simple and as obsolete as that D-Vision was, it tracked all of the flex file numbers. We put a window burn of the time code and the key codes on the tape. When it came time to print out our EDL (Edit Decision List) for the negative cutters, we were able to cross-reference the negative cutting list with the burned-in key codes and were amazed. We would lose a frame every now and again, but over a 100-minute film, the lists were almost perfect.

We gave a copy of the key number list and a window burn copy of the movie to the negative cutters and everything went perfectly. I have never used my Avid in this manner, but I do have the proper software, so I'm figuring that it'll do it just fine. As far as Final Cut Pro, I'll get back to you.

In an early film that I edited, the producers didn't use flex files. The camera original was transferred to tape to be edited on a computer and a work print was made. (Many Hollywood movies do this.) When it came time to have the negative cut for prints, I had to go through on a (flatbed) film editing machine and conform the work print to the video edit so that we could take the key numbers off the work print for the negative conforming. I had to "eye ball" the scenes from the video since I had no other reference. If we had flex files we could have avoided this extra work.

If you are finishing on tape, check the quality of your material.

There are some instances where you'll just dump it out of your computer and go from there.

With *The Gas Cafe,* I took the picture straight off the drives and went to a transfer house to do a tape-to-tape color correction. That worked well, but there were only so many things we could correct because the tape can only handle so much latitude since we weren't coming off the original tapes. If we would've gone back to the camera original and rebuilt the entire show from there on an Avid Symphony, or done it the way we did it for years in a traditional online editing suite, we could have made finer corrections. I didn't have the budget to do that.

In reality, I didn't have the budget to do a tape-to-tape correction, but Tim Maffia, (a good friend of mine) is a colorist. He convinced his bosses to let us do the correction on the day after Christmas, which was a weekend as well. The place wasn't booked so they figured, why not? Thanks again, Tim.

With *Kicking Bird,* I dumped everything onto two firewire drives, and I mean everything! I gave it to my friend Keith Rollinson (at Sector 550) who has Avid's Mojo, a color correction system. We color corrected the whole thing on the drives then dumped it out using his Avid Symphony, and mastered onto digital Betacam. I think it looks pretty good, plus we had a lot more flexibility in the color correction.

My Hairdresser's Brother Can Do Titles

When it comes to doing titles, there are as many options as there are software programs. In this regard, you're on your own. My only advice is don't make your titles flashier than your movie. I know you can do cool things in Photo Shop and After Effects and you probably have a friend who is pushing for that, but these are your titles! Unless your title sequence is critical to the movie, I say the simpler the better.

I work with a designer who always makes my titles fit the style of the movie. Jeff Pollard (POLLARDdesign) is amazing. I tell him what the movie is about. He asks a bunch of questions, and comes back with stuff that blows my mind. And it's in the style of the movie.

Jeff did amazing things on both *The Gas Cafe* and *Kicking Bird.* I bring Jeff in during rough cut screenings because he's a smart guy and has a good sense story-wise of what works and what doesn't. He starts thinking about the title design right then and there. It's a pleasure to work with a really smart designer.

I also have to say, in *Kicking Bird,* it was Jeff who came up with the graphics before the opening of the movie. He wrote them, chose the type style and showed me how he thought they should be used at the head of the movie with no sound. When we tried it, it blew me away. Remember, good ideas come from all sorts of places.

I also want to say this, about titles. *Birddog* has a full-blown opening title sequence, and for that movie, I think, it works great. The opening song and credits help set up the movie.

I had a discussion with a buddy during *The Gas Cafe* who said, rightly so, "Why have an opening sequence with titles to introduce actors we've never heard of? Nothing personal, Kel, but no one knows who you are either, and the world is not waiting for another Kelley Baker Film. Why not just jump into the story, and put all of your credits at the end?"

He was right. No one knows who you are, and they probably don't know your actors either. You've heard that phrase, "Cut to the chase?" Well, cut to the chase! Who needs some big opening title thing? Start the movie!

I do advocate having a few titles up front to let people know what's going on, but then get into the story. I'm so sick of seeing all these vanity fucking titles at the beginning of movies by people I've never heard of.

Angry Filmmaker's note: Many of the titles we see on Hollywood indie movies are there because of actors and their agents. They negotiate who comes first, how big, and other useless shit. Who cares who is in the damn movie? I want a good story! Wait a minute, those movies are about commerce, not art. I forgot.

And how many fucking "producers" does a film need, for crying out loud! I had better stop now, take my medication, and move on with the book.

Finally, after months, the picture is looking pretty good.

Sound Design for Independent Features

"It's the dialog, stupid."

Think about the films you've watched lately. How was the sound? Did you walk out thinking the sound or the music was really great? If you did, then the filmmakers FAILED!

You should walk out of a movie talking about the story. If you talk about anything else, the filmmakers blew it. Why? Because movies are supposed to be about storytelling. Not music, sound, special effects, cinematography not even acting.

If a movie has good sound, you shouldn't notice it.

If you heard lots of sound, that's not necessarily good sound.

As the sound designer on *Good Will Hunting, To Die For, Far From Heaven,* and *My Own Private Idaho,* I think they had the right sound. The sound reinforced the story. It didn't stand out. There are a lot of great moments in these films, and sound helps them, but sound doesn't take over. There's a big difference.

Ever watch the Academy Awards? I mean the technical awards.

You know, the ones most people talk over. Costume Design? Editing? Sound Editing? Do you know what films had the best sound in any particular year? You won't find that information at the Academy Awards. What you'll find are the films with the MOST sound.

You think I'm kidding, check it out. All the nominated films are huge blockbusters that are too loud. They overwhelm you with lots of explosions, fights, and sheer noise. That's not tough to do. Anyone can throw lots of sound at you and try to overwhelm you so you miss bad dialog and weak plots. For more information on bad dialog and weak plots, please see anything by Michael Bay, James Cameron, Steven Spielberg, Jerry Bruckheimer, the list goes on and on. But I'll stop now.

Loud movies are easy to do. The tough ones are the quiet ones. Think about *My Dinner With Andre.* Two guys talk in a restaurant. How do you make that sound interesting? Or at least not monotonous.

What about a movie like *Sideways*? It's two guys talking about wine and relationships. You have no big sounds to hide behind. The small realistic films are tough. Mostly because nothing happens, but it still has to sound real. I can't tell you anything about the sound in *Sideways,* but I can tell you about the story.

Of course, there are exceptions. A film like *Das Boot.* The sound designer made the submarine a character. Remember all the creaking? The rivets popping? Waiting for the depth charges to explode? Waiting for the explosions was worse than the explosions themselves. It was brilliant.

The sound helped create suspense. When they were stuck on the bottom, it seemed like days. You felt like you were on the sub with them. The music was pretty sparse which made the whole voyage unforgettable. Go see that movie! That's great sound. *Pearl Harbor? Titanic? Private Ryan?* Give me a fucking break! (Sorry Gary, just my opinion.)

Check out the opening to Sergio Leone's *Once Upon A Time In The West.* There are only a couple of (badly) dubbed lines in the first 12 minutes of the movie. Everything else is sound effects. No music, just effects. It's great; even without dialog, you know what's happening. Three mean, vicious killers are waiting at a train station in the middle of nowhere and someone is going to die. The West is really hot and boring, where water is an important commodity. The steam locomotive feels like a living, breathing thing, it's an important character. That's all we need to know.

Leone uses sounds like water dripping, a fly buzzing, and a squeaky wind mill to ratchet up the tension. You know these guys are evil by the way they're filmed and you know that they stink by the sound effects. Each one has a personality that is revealed through their movements, or lack of movement, and the particular sound associated with them.

The scene starts to feel a little monotonous at times, because they are just waiting. It's extremely hot, and they're waiting. We are shown boredom, but as viewers, we're not bored.

The opening is brilliant because it introduces many of the elements that reoccur in the rest of the film. Although I am talking about the great sound, the story, to me, is unforgettable as well. And Henry Fonda is the most amazing bad guy of all time. The sound and the visuals help tell the story, and Sergio Leone uses both to reveal character. On this movie, he and his crew were hitting on all cylinders.

Try doing a quiet movie. That's a challenge. Even if it's quiet, you have to have sound because we always hear things: wind, distant traffic, birds. The things in the natural world are always there, and when they're there we don't notice them. But take them away...

It makes the audience extremely uncomfortable. If you want to show an audience something bad is about to happen, let the natural sound fall away. Most people won't notice it, but something won't feel right. Then BAM! Disaster hits. Removing sound takes guts. Most people won't do it. In Hollywood, and in most films, they cue the music when something bad is about to happen. And it's the same cue over and over. People think when they hear music something bad is going to happen, and they start preparing for it. It's like Pavlov's dog.

That is the genius of Hitchcock and the original *Psycho.* Why was the shower scene so scary when it first came out? Because Janet Leigh goes into the shower and it's all natural sound. There was no music cue giving things away. It also helped that Janet Leigh was listed as one of the films stars, and in those days you didn't kill off a star so close to the beginning of the movie.

I love the shower scene because of its absence of music. It was just a mundane moment in someone's life, then BOOM! She's dead, and the audience has had their breath knocked out of them. Brilliant! There is no way they could have anticipated what was about to happen.

Check out any of Saul Zaentz's films. I still think *Amadeus* is a seamless movie. It's about music, and music that most people say they don't like, classical with some opera thrown in. I'm a hard-core punk, rock and roll, alternative kind of guy, and yet I am hypnotized by that film every time I see it.

Look at *The Right Stuff, Mosquito Coast, At Play In The Fields of The Lord.* Oh, just watch all of them. Those guys at Saul Zaentz's (former) Film Center had a way of using sound that totally supports the rest of the movie. Even in *Amadeus,* or should I say, especially in *Amadeus,* sound exists to move the story forward. This is something that most "sound designers" don't get, especially musicians who call themselves sound designers. But we'll get to that.

For all you wannabe directors out there and I'm going to keep saying this, first and foremost, hire a good location sound recordist, no matter what you do.

Angry Filmmaker's note: As a recovering sound designer, I would rather spend my time being creative than fixing shit. With bad original recordings, there's not much I can do. If a sound is on tape under dialog, you're stuck. Not even the best software program can remove a sound or even diminish it without altering everything around it. If you want your leading man to sound like an alto from the Vienna Boys Choir for a shot or two, that's your business, but I don't. You can cut and paste, loop, add voice over, or shoot yourself.

Why You Want to Hire a Real Sound Recordist

One of the most important things in any movie is sound. And the most important sound? It's the dialog, stupid! If you can't hear or understand the dialog, then you're hosed. You've got nothing. It doesn't matter how pretty your pictures are, how good the acting is, what a terrific music score you have, or how clever you think you are. If you can't hear or understand the fucking dialog, you've got NOTHING!

Those Lips Don't Look Right

A question I'm asked all the time is, "How much ADR do you

187

do?" ADR stands for Automatic Dialog Replacement, and there is nothing "automatic" about it. It is also called looping. It is where we replace bad location dialog with clean dialog recorded in a studio. One guy figured we ADR 80% of the lines (no shit!). He was shocked when I told him I rarely use ADR. If you hire a good location recordist, you won't need it. You don't want to use it. ADR IS A LAST FUCKING RESORT! Can I say it any clearer than that?

Why? Because ADR is not, and will never be, as good as the original audio take! The sound quality won't be quite right. The performance will be close but not as good. I know there's all sorts of new software that can match the words to the lips, but just matching the words to the lips is not what's important. It's the feeling of the entire scene.

I've worked with some great dialog and ADR editors and some great mixers who had tons of top quality outboard gear, and we really took our time to get everything right, and ya know what? The ADR still stands out like a sore thumb, to me. Even if it looks right technically, it just doesn't feel the same as the original.

The Magic of ADR

Think about it. If you're an actor, you're used to playing off other actors. On the stage, on sets, wherever. What we're asking an actor to do when it comes to ADR, is to come into a large room with a few chairs and a table or two. It looks nothing like a set. Then we're going to project a giant picture of him or her on a screen, not color corrected, with unfinished audio. We'll put headphones on them so they can hear the bad audio, and ask them to recall that feeling they were using as their motivation for an intimate scene that was shot months ago. Without anyone to play off of, we expect you to deliver a similar performance to the one in the film. We're all going to stare at them while they're doing it, and, oh yeah, "Can you match your lip movements as well?" Give me a break!

ADR is inferior.

If you are the director, you will always see the ADR and it will bother you every time you watch the movie. And you know what? It could have been prevented.

In some of the films I worked on with Gus Van Sant, and with my own films as well, if there is a line that's a little distorted, but it's a great take, I go with it. That's right, I use it. Why? Because usually, it's a line where the actor gets a bit out of control in their performance. The take is the best take there is, and sometimes it's because of a little distortion. I think it's great to use it. An occasional line works, and the audience forgives you, or doesn't even notice because it sounds real. Depending on the movie you're making, you want it to sound real.

Some actors are good at ADR, but many are not. Why rely on fixing something when a little distortion might add to the intensity? Let it go.

Angry Filmmaker's note: Which brings me to something that has always bothered me. It's the sentence, "We'll fix it in editing, post, the mix." Whatever. If you spend a little more time on the set and get it right the first time, you don't have to worry about wasting time and money on an inferior fix later on. And trust me, no matter how long you work on something in post-production, it will always bother you. Whenever someone says we'll fix it later - it's often said by a producer - I look at that person and realize I'm in the presence of an amateur. They don't know what they're talking about. All they want to do is move on because they think they're saving money. They're not.

189

They're idiots and don't belong on the set.

There are times when things do go wrong and they have to be fixed in editing, or sound, and that's fine. But recognize that it should be a last resort, not your first option.

I look at sound not as a sound designer, geek, or tech head. I look it as a filmmaker. When I write scripts, I hear the movie in my head. I hear music, sound effects, voices, radio waves (okay, not radio waves if I remember to wear my aluminum foil hat.), I already hear the movie. I know what is going where.

When I work on someone else's movie, I approach it the same way. As a filmmaker. What can I design and create as the sound designer to push the concept of the entire film forward?

So let me step backward and define what a sound designer does so there are no misconceptions.

WE ARE NOT ON THE SET!

We are rarely (if ever) consulted before, or during, the shoot. We don't arrive on the job until the damage is done. Traditionally, we come in during the rough-cut stage. We are supposed to "fix it in the mix." The first time I hear the sound is usually at a screening, although sometimes I do get called in before the first screening.

If it's a "Hollywood independent," I usually come in just before a preview screening and then I'm given a little time to do a quick sound cut and mix, usually less than two weeks for everything. Then the executives see it for the first time, along with a preview audience. This is a very stress filled two weeks. How these two weeks goes will determine how the rest of the job goes. If the last week goes well, everything will be fine for the next few months. If it doesn't go well, your life will be a living hell for the next few months. or you'll get fired before you have a chance to do anything.

We're Running Out Of Time, Tell Me Everything

Usually, I only get to watch the film with the director once. This takes five to seven hours because we are constantly stopping and starting the movie and talking. I want to know everything. Why did the director do what he or she did on the set? What do the various scenes mean in terms of character development? What does the background feel like to them? I ask as many questions as I can think of that relate to all aspects of the story and the characters. I usually fill an entire legal pad with notes.

I do this now, because it is the only time I'm going to get with the director until the mix. And the mix is a hell of a time to start asking about motivation and sound for individual characters.

Angry Filmmaker's note: The title "sound designer" has a very impressive ring to it, but in reality we are at the bottom of the food chain. By the time we come on, there's never any money left. Everyone else went over budget...

How does that happen? If the director needs special equipment for a shot or a scene that's not in the budget, do you think anyone is going to say "NO" to the DIRECTOR? When the shoot is behind schedule, or the director wants more days to shoot, what do you think is going to happen? They're going to go over budget.

When the movie is being edited and the director and the editor need a few more weeks or a special music cue that's not in the budget, guess what's going to happen? The producer says, "We'll take it out of post," and I hate that term as much as the old "We'll fix it in the mix."

Where do you think the money is going to come from? It's certainly not going to come from the negative cutter. Or from prints and advertising. No. It always comes out of the sound budget. Why? Because we have computers. How tough can it be to do sound? The location guy didn't need nearly as much time as the camera department, or art department, or props, or the cast, or anybody. So how tough can sound be? We're cutting your schedule and your staff. And the sound better be great "because you guys have computers."

Set Bullshit

The location sound guys always get the short end! How come it can take a day to dress a set, five hours to light a scene, and another hour to get the camera move right, but everyone screams at the sound people if they want a rehearsal for level check? And half the time, it's the fucking camera crew that's doing the yelling!

But that's not your problem. You have to fix the shit. So here's what you do.

Start complaining from the beginning about how bad the dialog was recorded. Whether it was or not. You need a scapegoat. It's the Hollywood way. Like anyone you're dealing with knows anything about sound. You tell them up front, "Everything is shit!" Everyone else dumps on the location sound people, why shouldn't you? You better hope you never actually meet the location recordist, because most of them are pretty nice people who get dumped on more than you.

After you have trashed the location sound people, there is nowhere to go but up.

So You Want to Be a Sound Designer

To be a good sound designer or filmmaker, start listening, every day, all around you. What does the world sound like? The sound of a room changes over the course of a day. If you're in a restaurant, is it breakfast time or lunch? What if it's that dead time, in the middle of the afternoon, before the old-people dinner specials. Every place sounds different at different times of the day. When does your scene take place. What's going on outside? Is it a busy street, or a country restaurant? What if your scene is in someone's home? Apartment or house? Night or day? Urban or rural? There are 20 questions for every location.

Use your imagination.

Software is Overrated

Let's talk for a minute about sound-editing software. I don't care about software or editing systems. Those things don't matter. It's your imagination. A piece of software is a tool. It's a hammer. What can you do with this software? That's what you want to know. Everyone now uses Pro Tools. It was never the best editing software, it was just the software with the best marketing department.

It's like the old Betamax versus VHS. Betamax was clearly superior in all aspects, but Sony would not release any of its proprietary stuff. So a few other companies banded together to come out with something cheaper, then flooded the market with it. We became stuck with an inferior system. No wonder everyone hated VHS.

Find some audio software you're comfortable using that can do what you need it to do, and go with it. Just know that sooner or later you're going to have to deal with Pro Tools.

Mr. Really Bad Example

Let me draw you a picture featuring one of my biggest sound nightmares. I was working on a low-budget independent movie, years ago. The producer and the director hired a location sound recordist who convinced them he had a lot more experience then he really did. He wasn't that good. There is a scene in a restaurant where the main characters are having a conversation. The restaurant is on a main street and it got really loud and really quiet during the shoot. They put the two main characters near the front windows of the restaurant so we could see what was going on outside.

The recordist booms the two actors, which is perfectly fine. The scene probably took a good part of a day to shoot. It was obvious one set of shots was done during the morning rush hour. Some close-ups were done during the lunch hour, while others were done during the late afternoon. I had three totally different sets of backgrounds outdoors to deal with as the editor cut from shot to shot.

The sound recordist apparently thought he was doing me a favor by hanging a separate mic outside the restaurant during filming so he could pick up the real backgrounds. Not a bad idea, but then he mixed all of the different mics (the actors and the background mics) onto a single mono track on his recorder.

I couldn't split anything out. I was stuck with all of the backgrounds on the dialog tracks. On one particular edit, we see a bus passing by the restaurant, but before it goes all the way through frame, the editor cut to another shot done at a

194

totally different time of day, with a very quiet background.

This scene was a mess! I had no money to do ADR, and the two young actors, I was told at the time, didn't believe in ADR. We spent days trying to clean up this scene and make it so you can at least understand what's going on. I can't stand to look at that scene to this day. The director always justifies the bad sound by saying it was the effect he was going for. He didn't want you to understand what was being said in a three-and-a-half-minute scene? That's director's bullshit! But hey, he's the artist, right?

Low Flying Objects

What do I do when I have some shots within a scene that have problems, like an incomplete bus pass by? In *Finding Forrester,* we had a small airplane flying overhead in Yankee Stadium for only a few takes.

Over the years I have put together a pretty large and fairly complete sound library. I go to it and get my own buses and airplanes. I lay my own effect across the offender on the dialog track. Then I lengthen it so I can ease the effect in before the actual take, and out over the next shot. What the audience hears is a bus smoothly going by, an airplane flying away. I will put in all sorts of effects to cover up the problems and try and make the whole scene feel natural.

Hide in Plain Sight

In a crowded office scene where I have jumps in the backgrounds between shots that I can't smooth out, I will cue up three phone rings. The first ring is just placed in the track to become part of the background, trying to make it unnoticeable. Then I use either the second or third ring to cover the offending cut. A phone ringing is a natural occurring sound in our world and most audiences will hear the first one, recognize it for what it is, a background sound, and tune it out when it occurs again the next couple of times. They totally miss the jumps in the backgrounds.

If you have a sound library, make sure you have lots of vehicle sounds, phone rings, and anything else you can think of to draw attention away from problems you have with the audio. Doing sound design is one part creative, one part fixing things other people fucked up, and one part creatively fixing even more fuckups.

Eventually, you will start getting to do creative sounds. There are some scenes in movies where creativity is the order of the day. In the remake of *Psycho,* I decided to make the house one of the characters just like what was done in *Das Boot.* Every time we are in the *Psycho* House, if you listen closely, you'll hear whispering and breathing, very lightly interspersed sounds that make it feel as if the house is alive.

I recorded a bunch of human sounds, then slowly and subtly brought them up in the mix. Just when you think you hear something, I bring the volume down again. I don't want you to know what you're hearing. I want you to feel as if something is going on. I have been told at some screenings that people had an odd feeling during the scenes in the house. A feeling that they couldn't really put their finger on. The house felt alive, and creepy. In my opinion, that sound design worked because you weren't hit over the head with it. People couldn't identify why the house felt creepy, it just did. My sound work didn't draw attention to itself.

You can use subtle sounds to create mood. You can manipulate sounds to get everything from a character's point of view. During the fight scene in *Good Will Hunting,* everything we hear is from Will's (Matt Damon) point of view. It's not realistic sound, although some of the elements are real; it's how he is perceiving the action around him.

Rent *All That Jazz.* There's a wonderful scene where the cast is doing a run-through of the new play and the main character (Roy Scheider) can't hear any of it. We hear his pencil breaking, his heart beating, and other sounds like that. It's an incredible look inside his head for that scene. It helps develop and reinforce his character.

Always think about reinforcing characters with sound.

Now, we've talked about ADR (DON'T DO IT!) What about foley?

What is Foley and Why Should You Care?

Here's everything you need to know about foley.

Foley effects are sound effects that are performed to picture. You project the movie in a studio and one or two people actually perform the sound effects while the picture is playing. The sound effects are recorded live and are used in the final movie.

The most common foley sound effects are footsteps and clothing rustle. Some effects are actually much easier to do in foley than cutting them individually. In *Finding Forrester,* there were lots of scenes with basketballs. The main character was a high school basketball player. It was much easier for us to have the foley artists do the basketball dribbling for the movie then to sync each basketball hit by itself.

Foley is used mostly when you have to deliver a foreign mix of your movie. You use foley footsteps when you can't use the footsteps on the production recordings because you have to remove the dialog so that it can be dubbed into whatever language a particular country uses.

We had the basketball effects on the dialog (or production) tracks which were in sync. If there was any conversation going on during any of the dribbling, then when it came time to deliver the foreign version of the sound mix, we couldn't use any of the production basketball effects that had dialog on it.

In the case of *Far From Heaven,* the Todd Haynes film, Todd wanted us to do all of the foley footsteps so they sounded like they came from a sound library that was put together in the 1950s. In fact, he wanted all of his sound to sound like it was from the 1950s and this was a studio picture. That was a challenge.

Angry Filmmaker's note: Any time you do a period film it's a challenge. I had to find telephone effects with bell ringers, typewriters, and real V8 automobile engines. Most sound libraries don't have these effects anymore. And finding the real thing can be tough.

As a sound designer, you learn to be resourceful trying to find some of these effects. We went out and recorded some old automobiles to get some realistic sounds of heavy old car doors closing. I mean, let's face it, a 55 Buick door certainly sounds a lot different from a Honda door.

But back to foley. If you're doing a small independent movie, the odds are you're not going to use much foley. With *Kicking Bird,* I did all of the foley myself with two of the effects editors, and we recorded it straight into the Pro Tools. I watched the movie on a monitor and performed the effects right in the editing room. I knew exactly what I needed, so I only did the

198

effects that were absolutely necessary.

Since I had decided all of the running sequences would be done to music, I didn't even worry about doing footsteps for the runners. That would have driven me crazy if I had to do all of that. I just figured out what I needed to get the job done and did exactly that. Since I was going to be doing some of the mixing myself, and after 20 years of doing it, I knew what I needed and didn't need.

Now that you're working on your dialog, cleaning it up, gathering and cutting your sound effects and foleying just the effects that you're going to need, don't you think it's time you put some music together as well?

Nightmare on Music Row

Now I don't know where this rumor got started, but you CANNOT use other people's music in your film without permission! I keep hearing of these stories about how you can use a certain amount of music without paying for it. That's bullshit! If you use music someone else has copyrighted, you have to pay for it, or at least get their permission. Length doesn't matter.

If the music is public domain, that's fine. But if it's been recorded, then the performance is probably NOT in the public domain! You will have to pay for the performance rights. If you rerecord it yourself, you should be okay.

I don't want to get into rights, clearances and all of that stuff here. That's not what this book is about. If you have music questions, talk to a fucking lawyer who specializes in this crap! If you want to know who owns rights to various songs call BMI or ASCAP. They should be able to tell you not only who wrote a tune, but who owns the rights and how to contact them or their agent.

Dumb Film Festival Music Trends

There is also a trend not to clear music for your movie if you're going to send it to film festivals to find a distributor. Then WHEN it's picked up for distribution you get the distributor to pay for the music rights. If anything, WHEN should read IF, because the odds are, it's not going to happen. A lot of distributors won't pick up a film if the music rights aren't cleared already. Music can cost a lot and some distributors expect you to pay for the music. It's not going to come out of their share.

I think it's a bad practice, because if you don't get a distributor, then what? You can't really sell the movie to video stores, NetFlix, or places like that. You're kind of stuck unless you go in and change the music and then remix the whole movie. That's not a great idea for a lot of reasons. It costs more money. It takes energy to go back in and redo a finished movie. And the movie sits around on your shelf not doing anything for you until you get it done. And between you and me, most of the time these movies don't get done.

I'm with the Band

It seems like everyone knows a musician. If you don't know one yourself, ask five friends of yours and the odds are, at least one of them is going to know someone in a band.

Use original music whenever possible. If you don't have much or any money, this is your best choice. Most musicians want their music in a movie because more people are going to hear their work, and no one knows what might happen to it after that.

Someone could hate your movie but love the music. Or they might like your movie and the music. Either way, it's a win-win situation. Also, if you have all original music, it gives you more distribution and marketing opportunities. You can sell both the DVD and a CD soundtrack.

I always make a deal with my musician friends. I have NON-exclusive rights to their music. I can use it for the movie and any marketing possibilities associated with the movie. They still hold the copyright. If they end up selling a song that you've used for a commercial, another movie, or whatever, they get that money, not you, unless you work out some other kind of deal. Basically, I only have permission to use the songs in the movie.

I also do soundtrack deals, which benefits everyone. I get a percentage of the CD soundtrack. In return, I sell it on the website, sell it on tour, and cross-promote it with all of the DVDs and anything else I might be selling from the movie.

When working with musicians, remember, it's their music but it's your movie. If the music doesn't work or isn't what you had in mind, tell them. Don't put in anything that you're handed because it's free and you don't want to hurt their feelings. It will haunt you.

There is a song in one of my films (I am not saying which) that is not what I wanted. It's totally wrong, but under the circumstances I had to use it, and it still drives me crazy. I don't like it. Never have. I tried to make the best of it at the time, but because of timing and my schedule, I was stuck. Never again! To this day, I've never said anything about it to the composer because I know he really likes it.

In *Kicking Bird,* I drove the music guys crazy because I knew what I wanted. I rejected a lot of good songs. I thought they were great, they just weren't right for this movie. I am thrilled with the ***Kicking Bird*** soundtrack. It's exactly what I wanted. So be particular. You've lived with this movie for a long time and you're going to be showing it all over the place. There are already enough mistakes and things you don't like in the movie, don't make it worse.

Music Is Not Sound Design

Let me also say this about musicians. They are not sound designers. No matter what they tell you. They should just stick to music and for God's sake, do not let them come to your sound mix. They're going to want the music louder! Even if it's a dialog scene and the music is way in the background, they will come up with all sorts of reasons why it has to be louder. They're usually wrong! I have seen both unknown composers and famous composers do this. It is all about them. Wrong. It's all about YOUR movie!

When it's time for the mix, make sure you have all of your elements prepared in advance. If you have a budget, you should mix your film in a studio or stage that's set up to mix motion pictures. A good sized mix board, lots of outboard gear and a good sized screen to watch it on.

You will be amazed at how much better your movie plays on a decent sized screen, with the sound coming together. I am amazed every time I start mixing one of my movies how much better it seems to play on a larger screen. Plus, it's really nice not to see it on an editing monitor.

It's The Dialog, Stupid

While you're mixing, keep telling yourself, "It's the dialog, stupid." Make sure it's coming through loud and clear. Also, don't fall in love with things like the surround speakers. Their use in *Apocalypse Now* was cool; don't let it go to your head.

I always mix for the center speaker. That's the most important if you're hoping for a theatrical release. In a theater all of your dialog and your main sound effects come from it. Sprinkle the backgrounds, pass-bys and music into the left and right channels and you're good to go.

If you can't mix in a real studio, don't let that stop you. A lot of us can't afford it. My recommendation is to do the best job mixing on your editing station, burn a copy, then go listen to it in a couple of different places. If you can con a theater owner or manager into letting you come in and listen to your mix and watch your movie on the big screen while you're still in the process of the mix, all the better.

You want to know how it plays in a big room. If there are any big holes or glaring mistakes, it's going to show through in the theater. The first time I saw *Kicking Bird* on a big screen at a run-through, it sounded great. Then I saw two shots where the boom slipped into the frame for a moment. Some people saw it, some didn't. I fixed it!

For me, the best part of doing my own films is that in the mix stage, no one is telling me what I can and can't do. I don't have to turn around and ask anyone if what I've done is okay. I'm mixing for myself. And in the process, I've blown speakers, pissed off Academy Award-winning mixers, and done things the way that I've wanted.

How Does This All End?

You are going to have all sorts of choices towards the end. Do I mix in Dolby Digital? Dolby SR? SDDS? DTS? Forget about it! All those cost money. If you have the money, do whatever you want. If you don't, go with a nice plain Dolby Stereo mix. I think it's still free.

Once you're happy with your mix, walk away. You've done everything you can do. To quote The Beatles, "Let it be."

You have other things to worry about, like getting it seen.

CHAPTER 12:

Festival Bullshit!

"Nothing says independent film like the Sundance Film Festival and Hollywood Stars. Bob, stick a fork in it! You're done."

You spend years trying to raise the money to make your movie. You kill yourself on the set trying to get things right. You work all night editing. You mortgage your house to finally scrape enough cash together to finish your movie, and guess what? The next step is to send it to someone you don't know.

They might screen it themselves, hand it off to a committee made up of people who have never made a movie, or give it to a bunch of interns. They're going to look at your film, reject it without telling you why, and you get to pay for the pleasure. What the fuck is up with that?

If I've said it once, I've said it a thousand times, I hate film festivals! I don't hate all of them, but many of them are a waste of time.

Angry Filmmaker's note: One of the things I have noticed over the years is a lot of the same people show up at the major film festivals and markets. These are trust-fund babies. They hang out at all the right places and socialize. Sometimes they have a film there they "worked on." many times, Not! You'll find them at Sundance, SXSW, Toronto, Venice, and the Independent Spirit Awards. Don't get me started on awards... I hate them. It's just another club. Don't believe me? Look at some of the nominees year after year.

Small Festivals for People Who Love Movies

I am not saying that all film festivals are bad. I like the small ones. Small cities, fun prizes, and low entry fees. They are great because they're usually run by people who genuinely love movies.

No glitz, just lots of movies. Maybe I am too hard on some festivals. I think many of them got their start for all the right reasons. But once a festival catches on, suddenly it becomes this exclusive thing.

Sundance is the prime example. I know, I pick on them a lot, but they're big (wealthy) boys, they can take it. Plus, if they're paying attention to what I'm saying, they are a lot more sensitive than I thought they were.

No Sympathy for the Devil

Every year Sundance gets thousands of entries and they take a very small percentage for the festival. My problem is with the features that usually get in. Most have some big Hollywood/Corporate Indie connection. They usually feature a couple of stars, a star making their directorial debut, the director or the producer is someone you've heard of, or worse yet, the wife or husband of someone you're heard of. Their budgets are in the millions, and many already have distributors.

If we all stopped sending our movies to Sundance they probably wouldn't even notice. They're too busy schmoozing with their pals in LA and NY.

Most of us fill out our Sundance application, write our check, and get our movies in before the deadline. There is a group of producers and producer's reps who know the programmers at Sundance and call them up and say, "We know we've missed the deadline, our movie is still in rough cut, but we have (place star name here), and it's really good. Can we show you the rough cut?" These are the films that usually get in! They don't have to play by the rules like the rest of us. What would Sundance be without any big stars and the press that follows them everywhere? Why, it just might make it another film festival.

Do you really think the main programmers at Sundance watch every movie that is submitted? That's what interns do. They probably have screening committees do a lot of the heavy lifting. The programmers are stars on the festival circuit, and with the distributors. They're too busy to watch most of the movies that are submitted.

In reality, Sundance receives thousands of submissions every year, for very few spots. Why bother?

In many instances, film festivals are just an extension of marketing. At worst, they are an extension of studio marketing. Some distributors will buy a movie if it has played at a lot of film festivals. They say it has a "built-in audience." So why have so many festival films gone down in flames when they were released? Maybe the "built-in audience" had already seen it at the festival.

Festivals don't mean shit! When I was starting out, I sent my first short to tons of festivals and it was rejected by everyone. That didn't stop it from getting into a PBS series of shorts and being aired nationally. The first night it aired, it was seen by a couple hundred thousand people and I WAS PAID to have it air.

Don't take this rejection shit personally. Most of these people at film festivals (especially the big ones) have an agenda. And if you're an unknown, then you're not part of it. This is especially true with features. Short films are less political.

Short Films Have Feelings Too

I do however, recommend sending short films to festivals. That's where you have a chance to get your stuff seen. Film festivals need shorts. They may call them filler, but they need them to round out programs. And that is why I tell people to make short films. They are easier to place in film festivals.

It's also why I say make SHORT films! If you can make films that are in the 3-to 9-minute range, festival programmers love them! They don't really want 30-minute shorts. I know, I know, your 32-minute short is brilliant and it's your calling card to do features. That's fine, but you probably won't place it in many festivals because of length.

If you're interested in a particular festival go to their website and check out what they've programmed for the last couple of years. Most festivals are programmed every year by the same people, and if you do your homework, you can get a feel for the kind of stuff they like.

Don't send your romantic comedy to an experimental festival (unless it's way out there). As in everything else with this business, do some homework on the Internet and you can narrow down where you send your stuff. Which ultimately will save you time and money and maximize your exposure.

Since many film festivals are now seen as money-making

propositions, there are a lot of festivals that <u>really</u> don't mean shit. Who cares if you are in one of them?

A friend of mine got his first feature into a festival in New York. It was one I had never heard of, which doesn't mean anything. He was really excited. He told me what the fee was to enter, which I thought was kind of high. Anyway, he went back there and went to the screening of the film that showed before his. The place was packed! People were having a great time during that movie. When it came time for his, everyone left. He said there were maybe three people sitting in the screening with him for his movie. The film before his? It was a local film and the audience was made up of cast and crew.

He didn't do his homework, and he didn't do any of his own publicity. I'm not saying this festival was a scam. But it sounds like they didn't do a hell of a lot of work promoting the films. I'm not sure if that festival still exists.

I had another friend who heard about a festival in Texas. He entered his rough cut because he was still editing and thought he could complete it in time. He didn't, but the festival said he could show his rough cut and he did. To a nearly empty auditorium. They charged him quite a bit to enter as well.

What the hell kind of a festival would let you show a rough cut that wasn't part of some workshop, panel discussion, or a special event screening? One that merely wants your money? This was a movie with lots of special effects that weren't completed. It was truly a "rough" cut.

Again, do your homework on festivals. Check out their websites. Contact some of the filmmakers who've had work shown there. Ask about screening facilities. How were they treated by festival staff? What kind of publicity did they get?

Remember, most filmmakers will piss and moan about something. The projectors weren't bright enough, I didn't do enough interviews, I didn't get a deal...

Cut through that crap and find out how the festival is run. Overall, how many people turn out for it? Is this the only festival in town? Is it a major one? Do they have sponsors? Who? National or local? What is the media coverage like? If a festival has a newspaper, radio or TV sponsor, then the odds are better the press will be pretty good and you can expect some good coverage.

Places like New York, Boston, Chicago, and yes, even Portland, have a bunch of film festivals each year. Figure out where each one stands in the pecking order. If it's one of the important ones, then go for it. If not? Then you pay your money and take your chances.

Welcome to the Jungle

If it seems like a good festival and you get in, then you have to work it just like any other screening. Send out your own press releases. Find out about the local media and contact them to see if they want to screen your film ahead of time. Would they like to interview you? Yeah, festival people are supposed to be doing this, and maybe they are. But they're promoting their festival and a lot of other films.

You are promoting YOUR film. And you can do it better than they can. Don't leave publicity and marketing to someone else. It's not their movie. Find out what they're doing, and then take up the slack.

You need to get comfortable doing this. Why? Remember what I told you earlier, that marketing people are lazy and want a simple hook? They'll make a few calls and try to place a story or two. If that doesn't work out easily for them, you're going to be on your own anyway. Get used to it.

You've Come This Far

That's the other thing. If you can afford to go to a festival, do it. But always ask if the organizers can put you up. It doesn't have to be a fancy hotel. I have spent many a night on someone's couch. The important thing is to be there and meet as many people as possible.

Not all of us can afford to go to festivals. We have jobs or other commitments. But the personal conversation with a member of the festival staff, or the programmers themselves, can help you move forward in this world. If you can't go to a festival, at least call them, thank them and have a short talk. You want them to remember you in a positive light for next year.

Your Film Sucks and You're a Failure!

Now if you have a feature, and you know that Sundance or SXSW is the festival that is going to make your career, and then you're rejected, all is not lost. There are plenty of other festivals out there. I'm sure you're saying that none of the other festivals have the reputation of those two, so why bother?

Ask yourself, why am I interested in getting my movie into film festivals in the first place? Is it so you can be discovered, get a huge advance, make a bigger movie with Miramax's money and sell out? Then you're right. None of the other festivals make sense. They're all inferior. But if that's what you want to do, then you've picked up the wrong book in the first place.

Angry Filmmaker's note: Why are so many filmmakers sitting

on their films and waiting until the Sundance deadline? I know
Sundance wants only US premieres, but unless you're a member
of the club, you are not getting in the door. We are the unpopular
kids, the poor ones. Fuck Sundance, and even Slam Dance.
They might have been good at one time, but not anymore.

The purpose of film festivals for Real Independents is exposure.
What happens after that is up to you. Not them. If you're going
to self distribute, then just about any film festival looks good on
your DVD cover. If you're trying to get your movie into
Blockbuster or Hollywood Video, then a major festival is better,
but there are a lot of places where you can sell your movie
without a major film festival win. It's just a little tougher, and
you have to be a better salesperson.

Don't ever let a film festival determine if your movie is any
good. Like I always say, "Fuck 'em if they don't like it!" If you
think it's good, then keep sending it out.

The Sophisticated Europeans

Depending on your movie, sometimes European film festivals
are better. I always console myself with the fact that Europeans
always discover things first. Europeans are smarter, well read,
and there is a lot to be said about a European film festival win.
You can always say, "The Americans just don't understand my
work." Hey, it's worked for a lot of filmmakers. And personally,
I would much rather get into a European festival than an
American one anyway. I think it looks better on your resume.

I'm sure that European film festivals have their own politics and
rules, but being so far away from them, we aren't as familiar
with their bullshit! Once again, do your homework. What films
have done well there? What American films have been in their
film festivals? Just about everyone these days has a website.

It's pretty easy to contact other filmmakers to find out how legitimate certain film festivals are.

Angry Filmmaker's note: When contacting other filmmakers always tell them up front you just want some information, not contacts! If people come to me who I don't know asking for contacts, I tell them to shove it! Information I'll give out. Names and phone numbers I won't! I have worked too long and too hard to get my own contacts and a level of trust with these people. I'm not going to hand stuff off to anyone who asks. Any smart filmmaker feels the same.

Festivals can be a necessary evil. And evil is the right word. We need them, but we need them to be much more open to different kinds of movies. Like movies made by Real Independents.

Let's Pretend It's an Angry Filmmaker World

In the case of Sundance? Blow it up! Start all over again. It was great in the 80s and early 90s. It was still a chummy little club, but at least it was much more open than it is now. Put a $200,000 limit on the budgets for any film in competition! Any movie with a star of any sort, films, TV, music, whatever, you're not in the competition. (They can be put in a sidebar series called, "Pretending They Are Independent.") Make the festival accessible to filmmakers who are struggling to get their work seen. Reserve rooms for poor filmmakers so they can afford to go. Make this festival about Real Independents again.

Same thing over at the IFFM (Independent Feature Film Market). They're no longer letting in many "completed movies." What's up with that? So you can show your rough cut to a distributor and they can tell you that you need to make a bunch of changes for free, and then they'll consider showing it? Fuck that! This is supposed to be about INDEPENDENT films. Not "sort of independent" films.

To make festivals really work again, they need to be about the films and the filmmakers. They're becoming too much of an event. They are getting bigger than their mission. I think that's a problem.

To all you programmers out there, make your festivals about the films, not about the festivals. "We come to bury Caesar, not praise him!" Make your festivals about the work, and showing films by filmmakers who probably won't get distributors, films that deserve to be shown and deserve to have an audience. Then maybe I'll write nice things about you.

The End
(Roll Credits)

RESOURCES

& Other Points of Interests

I really hate doing a list like this because like video cameras, parts of this list will probably be obsolete by the time this thing is published. So I am going to post this list on my web site as well. (Please feel free to drop me lines to update or add to it.)

So for what it's worth, here it is ...

Websites (and blogs) I like:

www.angryfilmmaker.com - - I have to blow my own horn...

www.POLLARDdesign.com - - Cool titles, logos, and graphics, plus Jeff is a buddy of mine who does all of my design. You better call him!

www.zoomcreates.com - - They designed and host my site. What can I say.

www.filmbaby.com - - Great film distributors, I use em!

www.showbizsoftware.com - - They have great software for contracts, budgeting, scheduling, you name it!

www.writebrothers.com - - Screenwriting software

www.indyfilmco-op.org - - One of my favorite websites for information on Independent film. Oh yeah, I also blog here ...

www.independentfilmsdirect.com - - Good features and articles

www.marklitwak.com - - Entertainment Law Resources - Mark writes a lot of good things that we all need to know.

www.warshawski.com - - Morrie Warshawski is great when it comes to fundraising stuff. Buy his books.

http://documentaries.wordpress.com/sponsorship-info/ - - Documentary sponsorship site.

www.mediathatmatters.org - - Progressive media stuff. We gotta support these guys!

www.gailsilva.com - - Gail Silva consults on documentaries and was the Executive Director of the Film Arts Foundation for many years. She is a true champion of Independents.

www.yourscreenplaysucks.com - - This is my buddy Will Akers. He's written a wonderful book.

www.filmaction.org - - A great non-profit film/video organization in Portland, Oregon.

www.swamp.org - - Southwest Alternative Media Project down in Houston. These folks are great for workshops and screenings.

www.bavc.org - - Bay Area Video Coalition.

www.911media.org - - 911 Media Arts Center in Seattle. Good screenings and work shops.

www.mewanthorsie.blogspot.com - - My favorite film related blog.

www.IFP.org - - The Independent Feature Project. They host the Independent Feature Film Market. A little too main stream for my tastes, but they can be a good source for information.

http://groups.yahoo.com/group/Oklahomamoviemakers - - Nice group of folks.

www.dcshorts.com/ - - This is the best damn short film festival out there. Jon Gann truly cares about films and filmmakers.

www.thewritersstore.com - - All of your writing needs.

www.celtex.com/overview - - all sorts of free programs for making movies. I have never used these but have friends who swear by them.

www.wga.org - - Writer's Guild of America

www.wgaeast.org - - Writer's Guild East

www.sag.org - - Screen Actors Guild

www.aftra.org - - The American Federation of Television and Radio Artists

www.ascap.com - - The American Society of Composers, Authors and Publishers (ASCAP)

www.bmi.com - - Broadcast Music, Inc

www.filmmaking.net - - There are all sorts of things here. Poke around for awhile.

If you want to make movies you have to speak the language.

www.filmsite.org/filmterms1.html - - Cinematic Terms

http://homepage.newschool.edu/~schlemoj/film_courses/glossary_of_film_terms/glossary.html - - Cinematic Glossary from the New School. This is a great list.

www.filmterms.com - - Film Terms by Tim Moshansky

www.everything2.com/index.pl?node_id=436819 - - Filmmaking Terminology

Books I like, or think you need to read!

In the Blink of An Eye by Walter Murch

On Directing Film by David Mamet

True and False by David Mamet

Film Technique and Film Acting by V.I. Pudovkin

Film Form (a collection of essays) by Sergei Eisensten

Film Sense (a collection of essays) by Sergei Eisenstein

Screenplay: The Foundations of Screenwriting; A step-by-step guide from concept to finished script by Syd Field

Your Screenplay Sucks! 100 Ways to Make it Great by Will Akers

The Screenwriter's Workbook by Syd Field

The Writer's Journey by Christopher Vogler

The Anatomy Of Story by John Truby

Film Scriptwriting : A Practical Manual by Dwight V. Swain

Stealing Fire from the Gods by James Bonnet

Script Supervising and Film Continuity, Third Edition by Pat P Miller

Filmmaking for Dummies by Bryan Michael Stoller & Jerry Lewis

A-Z Guide to Film Terms by Tim Moshansky

Filmmaker's Pocket Reference, The by Blain Brown

Lighting for Digital Video & Television by John Jackman

The Filmmaker's Handbook: A Comprehensive Guide for the Digital Age by Steven Ascher, Edward Pincus

The Complete Independent Movie Marketing Handbook by Mark Bosko (I learned a lot from this book, and Mark is a really nice guy.)

The Insider's Guide to Independent Film Distribution by Stacey Parks

The Practical Art of Motion Picture Sound by David Lewis Yewdall

All I Need to Know about Filmmaking I Learned from the Toxic Avenger by Lloyd Kaufman

And don't forget to check out a few film magazines.

www.filmmakermagazine.com - - Filmmaker Magazine
www.moviemaker.com - - Moviemaker Magazine
www.screenreport.com - - Southern Screen Report
www.Independentmagazine.org - - The Independent

If you find mistakes, or want to add more places please check out my web site, www.angryfilmmaker.com, and drop me a line. I want to try and keep some of these things up-to-date.

219

Made in the USA